PIGEONS, MARKS, HUSTLER'S

and Other Golf Bettors You Can Beat

By Sam Snead
and Jerry Tarde

Illustrations by Andy Myer

A Golf Digest Book

Published by Golf Digest/Tennis, Inc.
A New York Times Company
5520 Park Avenue
Box 395
Trumbull, Connecticut 06611-0395

Trade book distribution by
Simon and Schuster
A Division of Simon & Schuster, Inc.
Simon & Schuster Building
Rockefeller Center
1230 Avenue of the Americas
New York, New York 10020

First printing 1986
Manufactured in the
United States of America
Cover and book design by
Rich Gaipa and Karen Fecenko-Lyon
Jacket photos by Dom Furore
Printing and binding by
R. R. Donnelley & Sons

Library of Congress Cataloging-in-Publication Data

Snead, Sam, 1912–
    Pigeons, marks, hustlers and other golf bettors
you can beat.

    "A Golf Digest book."
    Includes index.
    1. Golf—United States—Betting.   I. Tarde, Jerry.
II. Title.
GV979.B47S63   1986   796.352'0973   86–19516
    ISBN 0–914178–69–5

Table of Contents

Preface

S ince we started work on this book about four years ago, Sam Snead has retired from competitive golf a minimum of six times. Like Sarah Bernhardt, though, he keeps taking curtain calls. If there is a secret to his longevity, it may be that Sam has played golf virtually every day since Woodrow Wilson was President. He just cannot help himself. When he isn't playing for tournament purses on the Senior PGA Tour, Snead usually can be found today playing $5, $10 and $20 nassaus at Pine Tree Golf Club in Boynton Beach, Fla., or at the Upper Cascades Course in Hot Springs, Va., or somewhere in between where the backswings are fast and the wallets are fat.

During one juncture of our research I met Snead at a senior event in Massachusetts to do some taping. He shot a 68 in the first round to tie Arnold Palmer for the lead and afterward held a press conference.

"Is this the first time you've shot your age since you turned 70?" asked one reporter.

"No," replied Sam, "I had a 65 and a 67 last week in Hawaii."

"Was that in competition?"

"I was playing for a little something, if that's what you mean."

Sam does not play golf unless it is for a little something. But one of the interesting restrictions he put on this book is that I was not allowed to use the word "gambling" in his presence. At first I thought it was a life-long fear of internal revenuers—that one day after publication a plain-faced fellow in a gray suit would show up and demand income taxes on every nassau he ever won, and he has not lost many. Then it occurred to me that Snead actually never has gambled. He has engaged in betting, but not once that I know of was any bet he's ever made a gamble. He always has the edge; his opponent knows he has the edge, and he knows he knows.

Getting a fair advantage is what this book is all about. In putting Snead's match-playing strategy into a whole philosophy of betting, I had to rely on some of my own less successful experiences to, sort of, cement his ideas together. For this reason I am indebted to all the boys who beat me in golf matches and card games while growing up on a municipal course in Philadelphia called Juniata, where for a time I was the "assistant pro." Actually my main responsibilities were to hose down the carts, sweep out the shop and sell chances to the punchboard—all of which earned me the nickname, "Pro Shop Jerry," and $96 a week. I owe special thanks to Joe Hunsberger, the late golf professional who hired me, and to my parents, who financed my education on and off the golf course.

I would also like to thank all the Juniata hotshots who are now driving Cadillacs that I made payments on: The Bear, Bigfoot, Trader Joe, Cash-N-Carry Vince, Jack Scats, Joe Cool, Hearin' Aid Bob, Bow Tie, Bucky, Wawa, Mother Lynn, Rube, Mr. Wonderful, The Rev. Moonhead, Snapout 1 and 2, Al the Baker, Pete the Fireman, Good-Time Charley, Plucker, Stuffy, Tombstone Paul, Stiff-Arm Freddie, Longhair, Mandrake, Plaster of Paris Paul, Chief Longball, Ritter, Mel the Cop, Jonas, Caddie Ed, Lefty Jerry, Rocky, Buddy Guys, Ben Higman, Frank Ferguson, Danny the Weasel, Butch, Wesley, Apples, Crazy Joe, Cosmo, Sparrow, Cholly Binoculars, Bounce and Dr. Strange Glove.

Sam and I also would like to thank Johnny Gazzolla and The Homestead, the resort that Snead represents in Virginia. We are also indebted to the patience, hard work and good offices of Paul Menneg, Larry Sheehan, Nick Seitz, Jack McDermott, Pam Mouat, Hillary Common, Lois Hains and all the editors of *Golf Digest*.

JERRY TARDE
Rowayton, Conn.

Introduction

I am no high-stakes gambler on the golf course. I'd like to make that clear straightaway. I probably don't bet any more than you do. At times I have played for a lot of money—when the circumstances were just right—but my normal bet is a $5 nassau six ways. By that I mean we're playing $5 on the front nine (one way), $10 on the back nine (two ways) and $15 on the 18-hole match (three ways). I like this better than the standard four-way nassau, with the back nine worth $10 and the front nine and the 18 each worth $5. It never seems fair to me if I beat you 4 down on the front and lose the back 1 down that I end up all even for the day.

I remember we were playing one of these six-way nassaus not long ago at the Upper Cascades Course in Hot Springs, Va. To keep it interesting, we also had "automatic 2-down presses," which simply means that whenever you go 2 down, an additional match, called a "press," starts on the next hole. Those $5 bets can really add up if you get a hot hand, and this summer day I was playing like a wildcat with his tail on fire.

First, let me back up and explain that I'd just got a tip from watching a baseball game on television a couple of nights before. The announcer kept pointing out that a hitter was not extending his arms to put the wood on the ball; he said the batter was keeping his arms in too close to his body. I said to myself, "Hell, it's like playing golf. Both your arms should extend through the ball." That's exactly what I hadn't been doing. So the next day, I go out and hit practice balls trying to extend my arms. I had those balls landing in a pile on the practice fairway like a stack of apples in a grocery store. And the next day I'm playing this match.

I was 70 years old then, and I've never had a day like that before or since. Every shot went like an arrow at the hole. I mean, it was the easiest round of golf ever played. I didn't come close to missing a shot.

On the first hole I hit a driver and a wedge and had a kick-in birdie. On the second hole, a par 5, I was on in two and just missed the eagle from 25 feet. I had what would be my longest birdie putt of the day on the third hole, 25 feet straight uphill, and it just fell out of the hole. On the fourth, I made a seven-footer for a birdie. On the fifth, I made it from five feet. Then I holed one from 20 feet for a birdie on the sixth. On the eighth, I left a 15-footer dead in the middle short. Then I made an eight-footer at No. 9, which gave me a 30 for the front nine.

On the 10th, I made it from seven feet. On the 11th, from six feet. Both were birdies. Then I missed an eight-footer for an eagle at 12. By this time, the guys I was playing against forgot about the match and started rooting for me, even though it was costing them money. Well, I cannot think of a finer position to be in: I'm collecting hand over fist and my pigeons are lapping it up.

I birdied the 13th from six feet and the 14th from 10 feet. On No. 15, I had it about 13 feet, and one of the guys had a putt along the same line so I saw the break, but I still missed mine. I never could putt. I thought I missed the birdie at the 16th, but it broke right into the hole; it was about 12 feet. On the 17th, I missed a 10-footer that went right around the hole. So I knew I needed a birdie on 18 for a 59. I hit a second shot that was going right at the flag—it sang "The Star-Spangled Banner" all the way—but the ball took a funny bounce to the right and left me about 22 feet away with a three-foot break. I didn't want to be too bold and three-putt, because two putts for a 60 would tie my nephew J.C. Snead's course record and that would be sweet. So what did I do? I kind of half-assed hit it and the putt broke off below the hole. Still, I had me a perfect 60, with 17 full shots and 13 putts on each side. I missed only one fairway (when the ball bounced through a dogleg), never missed a green and hit two par 5s in two.

It felt so good that I almost told the boys to forget the money they owed me. Then they came into the clubhouse and dropped the cash on the table. I guess seeing all that greenery brought me back to my senses.

People ask me all the time how I've kept up my interest in playing golf after all these years. I tell them, it's like Willie Sutton says: that's where the money is. I never get tired of ringing the cash register. But seriously, I love the competition. It's those head-to-head matches that keep me going.

You're probably a little surprised to learn that I'm just a $5 bettor. I've bet more on occasion, as I'll tell you about later, but whether I'm playing for $5 or $5,000 or the U.S. Open I always try just as hard. If there's a secret to my longevity in this game, besides God's blessings, it's that I never quit playing and I never stopped trying.

The longest I ever put my clubs away was when I went on a safari in Africa with a friend of mine named Gordon Fawcett. I just wanted to relax away from the game for a couple of weeks. Unbeknownst to me, Gordon brought his clubs. Before long I got tired of the jungle and started missing my golf. Gordon then produced his clubs, but the trouble was he forgot to bring golf balls. We quickly figured out that the closest thing to golf balls on the Dark Continent was dried elephant droppings. So we dug some holes in a cleared area of the jungle and played ourselves a little $5 nass. I had to give Gordon handicap strokes, but I beat him anyway because I insisted on playing "winter rules." You see, by being able to "lift, clean and place"—as they say on tour—I could reposition the dropping so I'd hit it on the firmer side. Gordon never caught on to this trick, and his kept disintegrating on impact.

There's always a trick to winning any game and golf is no different. The key is to recognize an opening and then make it work to your advantage. Some people call these tricks "turning points in a match." They're not always as obvious as finding the firmer side of an elephant dropping, but the results can be just as dramatic. What I hope to do in this book is to show you a few of this old dog's tricks, so you might make them work for you. It's amazing how much more fun golf is when you're winning than when you're losing. I just hope these tricks of mine will help you enjoy the competition, win more matches and keep ringing the cash register.

SAM SNEAD
Hot Springs, Va.

1

The Fun of Competition

I 've always been pretty competitive, even as a youngster. I guess you have to be with four older brothers and a sister and not enough meat to go around the dinner table. We were poor mountain folk. My father, Harry, was a big Dutch-German with a bushy mustache who worked in the boiler room at The Homestead and served as captain of the hose-and-reel brigade of the Hot Springs Fire Department. My mother, Laura Dudley, was 47 years old when I was born. I damn near didn't get here. But they don't make women like her anymore. She could roll a barrel of flour—which weighs 192 pounds—onto her knees and then throw it on the buckboard of a wagon. When I got to know what a momma was, she was an old woman. When I was 13, she was 60. I remember in high school, I used to dig potatoes in the garden about 75 yards from the house. I'd put two bushels of potatoes in a sack and my mother would come down and pick up the sack and carry it back to the house.

"Now, Mom, leave that alone. I'll carry it," I'd say.

Hell, she could have put me on top of the sack and carried it. Both my mom and dad died when they were 75. But I had plenty of kin who lived a lot longer. My great-grandmother was the best cornshucker in the Alleghenies at 90 and lasted to 106. And my mother's sister almost made it to 90 after having had 20 children.

The one kinfolk who probably taught me the fun of competition was my mother's brother, Ed Dudley. I called him "Unk." We used to pitch horseshoes in the backyard and bet ice-cream sundaes. He'd cheat like a bandit, but I'd still beat him. He would measure from the top or the bottom of the peg, as it suited him, but it was always opposite of what favored me. I remember one time he threw a ringer on the last pitch, and I said, "You know, Unk, if I throw one on top of yours that's a double score for me." He just nodded. Don't you know, I threw a ringer and he chased me all around the house.

One time I mowed down the grass in our backyard and sunk tomato cans about the size of a golf hole into the ground. It wasn't good enough to putt on, but we used to chip there. When Unk would come over on Sunday afternoons, I'd always try to hornswoggle him into a game. He picked up an old set of clubs from somewhere, with wooden shafts nailed together, half right-handed and half left-handed. One day he showed up and said, "Let's go over to the real course in town. I'll play you for the biggest chocolate nut sundae in the drugstore."

So we went over there to play. On the first hole, I said, "Unk, what did you have?"

"Damn you," he said, "I had a 5."

"No, you didn't," I said. "You whiffed a couple."

"Boy, don't you know a practice swing when you see one?"

"Yeah, but you grunted each time. You don't grunt on practice swings."

I had a hard time beating him at golf, because he couldn't count above five. But I beat him at everything else, including his favorite sport —fishing. The best time was when we had a bet for catching the most fish. Unk had staked out an old rock in the fishing hole where he knew they were hiding. He headed straight for it and started pulling them in right away. It didn't take me long to see what was happening. I climbed onto a big, old log and gave it a push toward Unk on his rock.

"Get off that log before it goes under and takes you with it," he hollered.

Just as it got near him, I jumped off the log onto the rock. "You don't mind if I catch your fish?" I said.

"Damn you," he said. "If you catch my fish, I'll scrub your head."

Of course, I started pulling them in like I had a net. "You just have to jiggle the line a little," I told Unk.

"I'll jiggle you," he said, scrubbing my head. To this day, I think all the head scrubbing he gave me is why I went bald. But I think he thought as much of me as he did of his own kids. And he sure taught me the fun of competition.

2

How to Pick a Partner— and Keep a Friend

I 've always believed that the ideal partner is the best player who looks the worst. Take for instance the time Chandler Harper and I agreed to play a practice round with Bob Goalby and Dow Finsterwald just before the Golf Digest Commemorative Pro-Am at Newport, R.I. Bob and Dow are at least 15 years younger than us, and Chandler is always suffering from one ailment or another, but he's a good, tough competitor not to be underestimated.

This day we get on the first tee and Harper is complaining about his bad back. "Sam, I can't bend over," he says. "I don't know if I can play. Could you tie my shoes?"

Now Bob and Dow are looking at each other and acting all concerned. "Hey, my partner is in bad shape," I say. "We need some weight. Give Chandler two strokes a side to make it an even game, and we'll play you a $5 nass."

Well, they jump at it like two old hounds going for a pork chop. Chandler's back got better in a hurry. He made six birdies and I made seven. We shot 60 better ball, 56 with the handicap strokes. Dow sidled up to me on the back nine and said, "You cheating SOB." I said, "Dow, how was I supposed to know Chandler would make a quick recovery?" That was one of the sweetest 20 bucks I ever collected.

Another time when appearances were deceiving involved a match set up by Dutch Harrison, a tour pro who hustled on the side. He and his partner had been beating a couple of fellows regularly when Dutch decided to go for the kill. His partner was a low handicapper but not in Dutch's class, so Dutch told him to stay home on this particular day. Then Dutch imported Herman Keiser from out of town; this was before Keiser won the 1946 Masters and became well known. On the morning of the big match, Dutch dressed Herman in overalls and had him sit in the caddie pen.

"My partner's sick today," Dutch told his pigeons. "He can't play, but I do believe I could beat you guys with a caddie for a partner."

"Take your pick," said his opponents pointing to the motley gathering of bag carriers.

"Hey, you, the skinny one, do you play golf?" Dutch said to Keiser.

"I play a little," said Herman.

"You're my partner today."

Keiser shot 67 on his own ball and they beat their opponents every which way. As the pigeons handed over the cash, one of them said, "That's the best goddam caddie I've ever seen in my life!"

My philosophy of picking partners is fairly simple.

Rule 1: Take the best player. Generally, the lowest handicapper isn't giving enough strokes, and the players getting strokes aren't getting enough. If you're playing a strange course, try to grab the host member as a partner. The home course advantage is often enough to make the difference.

Rule 2: Pick a partner whose personality is compatible with yours. You need to get along with the guy for four hours or so on the golf course. Compatibility is especially important if you're playing over several days, say in a four-day member-guest.

Rule 3: Never fight with your partner; just find another partner. I always said, only a fool argues with a skunk, a mule, a cook or a partner in golf. Henry Longhurst, the great British writer (and pretty decent player), had a good attitude on the course. He would take his partner aside on the first tee and say: "I just want you to know that I'll be trying like hell today. It may not look like it sometimes, but I'll be trying." That leads to my next rule of thumb in partner relations.

Rule 4: Don't apologize. The old pro Horton Smith had the right idea. Paul Runyan tells me that when he and Smith were partners, Smith would shake his hand before they started, tell him how glad he was to have Paul for a partner and then say, "I'm apologizing right now for any mistakes that I make today, but this is my last apology. Now let's go out there and do our best."

Rule 5: Choose a partner who hits the ball about the same distance as you do. When I was captain of the Ryder Cup team, I paired together pros who drove the ball similar distances; that way they could help each other with club selection. It's always good to have a second opinion on what club to hit, and I know from playing myself that I learned a lot more from a partner who was a long hitter like me than from a short hitter.

Rule 6: Bet your opponents, not your partner. Never make a side wager with a teammate; you end up pulling against one another to the detriment of the team. No matter how badly your partner is playing, try to be as encouraging and complimentary as possible. Good partners keep their egos in check. I don't know if this was their problem, but I do know that Ben Hogan and Byron Nelson couldn't beat anybody as a team. They seemed to play one another instead of their opponents.

Rule 7: Partners should have different playing styles. If you're an aggressive player, you don't want an aggressive partner. The best teams are made up of a bold player and a conservative one. Jack Nicklaus and Arnold Palmer are good examples of this. They don't come any more conservative than Jack, and Arnold is always charging up San Juan Hill. But together they won four World Cups (1963, '64, '66 and '67) and three national team titles (1966, '70 and '71). Of course, it didn't hurt that Jack and Arnie were the two best players in the game at the time, but that just goes back to Rule 1.

Rule 8: Stay away from hotheads. While you don't want a happy loser as a partner, the surgeon general says club-throwers are dangerous to your health. Avoid partners with low boiling points; their bad temperaments sometimes rub off.

Rule 9: Pick a partner with a winning attitude. Don't interpret that to mean a fellow with a .44 Magnum in his golf bag. A winner isn't necessarily a killer, but he's a little tougher when he has to be. And he's never careless. Get rid of the partner who after making a 6 on a stroke hole says, "Gee, I forgot I had a stroke there."

Rule 10: Keep a sense of humor in team play. Dave Marr told me one time he had a partner with a bad disposition who was having a bad day. After hitting a hook into the trees on one hole, he said to Dave: "Your foot moved. You moved your foot on my backswing."

"That's right," said Dave. "First I move this foot. Then I move that foot, and the next thing you know I'm walking." And that's just what Dave did, and he kept walking away from his partner down the fairway.

A study of handicapping and matchmaking by the U.S. Golf Association has concluded that you should never select a partner whose handicap is the same as yours. This makes a lot of sense if you think about it. You want your partner to get strokes on holes where you don't get any, so the best kind of team is composed of a relatively low handicapper and a high handicapper. *Golf Digest* magazine published a story on the USGA's findings entitled, "Grab a Partner with a 20-Handicap Who Can Reach the Par 3s" (by Ross Goodner, September 1984). It revealed, in part:

"Dean Knuth, the USGA's director of handicapping, says the average handicap is 17 for men, 31.5 for women. A golfer's average handicap differential (adjusted score minus USGA course rating) is 2.5 strokes higher than his handicap, according to Knuth, and 85 percent of all golfers average 1.5 to 3.5 strokes over their handicap. In other words, if your handicap is 17, your average score is probably 89 to 91.

"From these statistics Knuth has determined that there are three basic types of golfers:

"1. Steady Eddie—A fairly short but straight hitter who is deadly around the greens. His last 20 scores don't vary by more than five or six shots, and his handicap is only about one stroke below his average. Steady Eddie is strong in match play because he usually plays close to his handicap. He is not strong in stroke play because he rarely beats his handicap, and not by much if he does.

"2. Wild Willie—A long and inaccurate hitter who is not deft around the greens. His scores vary by perhaps as much as 20 or more strokes over his last 20 rounds. His handicap is often four or more strokes lower than his average. Wild Willie is strong in stroke play because on occasion he has great potential to beat his handicap by a lot. He is weak in match play because his variability has caused his handicap to be well below his average performance.

"3. Average Andy—A player who is neither unusually long nor exceptionally straight, whose handicap is about 2.5 strokes below his average score, who is about as strong in match play as in stroke play—who is, well, average.

"In general, then, a Steady Eddie should look for a Wild Willie as a partner to give the team potential. Wild Willie has a chance to reach the long holes in regulation. Steady Eddie gives the team stability, getting pars to offset his partner's disaster holes.

"The USGA recommends that in tournament play there be no more than eight strokes difference between the handicaps of the partners in order to make the competition fair. However, there are no rules in your weekly nassau, so you should try to find a partner whose handicap is at least 10 strokes higher or lower than yours."

Of course, nothing is guaranteed. The USGA won't pay your debts if you feed all this information into a computer to pick your partner and still wind up a loser. But at least you're giving yourself the best chance.

I remember I played Wild Willie to Paul Runyan's Steady Eddie in a practice round before the 1950 PGA Championship at Scioto Country Club in Columbus, Ohio. We went out by ourselves as a twosome and, on the sixth hole, met up with a couple of fellows I'd never heard of named Pete Cooper and Skip Alexander. We later became good friends on tour. But naturally, thinking Paul and I had the edge, I propositioned those boys for a little match. We had 12 holes left, so we played a $5 six-hole nassau. Paul and I were eight under par for those 12 holes, and we lost four ways, $20. They were 10 under. Afterward Runyan said to me: "Sam, as much as I hate to lose, I didn't mind losing today because you were so sure we were going to pluck those birds. It served us right." Even I had to laugh at that one.

3

How Much to Play For

I've always believed in playing golf for a little something, even if it's just 50 cents a side. There's nothing more boring than a walk in the park with three other guys. For me to play a casual round of golf with nothing at stake is a waste of time. I'd just as soon be down in the woods watching the squirrels.

When I first got acquainted with golf as a caddie, I learned to chip and putt with one club, playing for pennies and nickels and dimes in the caddie yard. We'd sneak out on the course and play a few holes with just one club, running to keep ahead of the law. That's how I learned to play a lot of different shots. More important, playing for money taught me to try on every shot. If I missed one, I'd lose a nickel that I might not have.

When Lee Trevino came out on tour, he was quoted as saying that the pressure of playing for somebody else's money in a tournament is nothing. "Real pressure," he said, "is a $5 nassau with $2 in your pocket."

No truer words were ever uttered by a Mexican, but the longer Lee stayed on tour, the bigger the nassau bet became. "Every time I see that story, the money increases," Lee told me. "Now it's up to $100 nassau with $20 in my pocket. I've played a lot for $25, but when you start playing for $100, you're going to start losing friends. I really believe that, and I don't have that many to lose."

My brother Homer used to live in Newport News, but he liked to play golf with his old cronies at the Upper Cascades in Hot Springs, which was about 250 miles from his home. He'd drive all the way up there in the morning, play 36 holes, pulling his cart, and then drive back that night. Now that is liking your golf, right? He always had the same foursome that would play $5 nassaus. Then they got a little smart and raised the ante to $10, then $20, then $30. Now when I saw him, all he'd do is complain about the other guys: "That so-and-so, boy, he put it on me today. You won't believe where that son of a buck moved his ball."

I said, "Homer, you know you aren't getting any fun out of golf anymore. You're coming all this way, and all you're trying to do is make a living off your friends. And if you lose, you're mad and drive home cursing."

"But they're doing things they never did before," he said.

"What you ought to do is go back to playing for what you can afford. Then you can laugh about it and if you win $20, all right, and if you lose $20, it's not going to kill you."

Once you play for a lot of money against friends, all of a sudden they're not friends anymore. I figure that if you go above a $5 nassau, you have to look at the other guy's hole card—and that doesn't promote friendship. So my advice to you: ALWAYS play for something, to keep your mind on your business, but NEVER play for more money than you have in your pocket.

Personally, I've stuck to this philosophy all my life. I've always been a $5 nassau bettor, once in a while $10, but rarely more than $25.

The most money I ever won in a golf bet started with a $5 nass. A friend of mine came up to me one day at Boca Raton and said, "Sam, I'd like to have a game." I said, "I'm all booked up till Tuesday. Come back then."

This was Saturday, and sure enough he comes back Tuesday with another fellow.

"My fee to play a round is $100 plus the cart or caddie," I said.

They agreed and we played for $5. With all the presses, I ended up winning $45 and we go in the clubhouse for lunch.

"Tell you what I'll do," I said. "I will dispose of the $100 fee and we'll play for a little something more."

They were all for that. My friend was a 5-handicapper, and his buddy was also a 5, and we picked up a car dealer who was an 8. We played another 18 that afternoon and I won about $700.

"Don't go away," they said. "Let's play some more."

So I canceled my lessons for the week, and we went on a tour of Florida courses: Palm-Aire, Pompano, Fort Lauderdale Country Club, Tamarack and a couple of others. I gave them all their full handicaps and kept beating them every day. But it never seemed to discourage them; they just kept pressing and raising the ante. The worst round I had was a 67, and I set four course records that week. I won $10,000 in seven days, and it all started with a $5 bet. This friend of mine lives out in Idaho now, and I still go over to see him every once in a while. We're still friends because he could afford to lose that much.

Probably the strangest thing I ever played for was a set of automobile tires. A fellow named Thompson, who was a big shot at General Tire, wanted to bet me I couldn't break 70.

"A set of Double Eagles?" I said.

"You're on," he said.

Well, I went out and shot 18 straight pars for an even 70, so we tied. The next time we played I said, "That game still on?" And he said OK. I had a 64 that day.

"Sam, it was a pleasure just watching you," he said. "I'll have those four tires shipped to your home."

"Four?" I said. "Where I come from, a set of tires is five. You got to have a spare, don't you?"

Mr. Thompson agreed finally, but it took a little convincing. I've always been known to have a close relationship with a dollar, so I'm accustomed to being kidded about it. They used to say Walter Hagen was the first man to make a million dollars in golf and spend it all, and Sam Snead was the first to make a million and save two million.

I wasn't the only one of my peers to have a high regard for money. Of course, we grew up at a time when nobody had any. I'll always remember Dutch Harrison losing a $5 bet to a guy he thought was an easy mark.

"Dutch, this is really an honor," said the man. "I'm going to frame this bill."

Harrison quickly grabbed back the fin and said, "In that case, I'll write you a check."

Chandler Harper, another pro of my vintage, always liked to play for a few dollars, but he had his limit. When he was just a boy, a professional gambler took a liking to him and offered him some pretty sound advice.

"Son," he told Chandler, "when you go around to tournaments and you see gambling going on, like craps games in locker rooms, don't get excited about all that money. Anytime you see a lot of money, one or two fellows are always there to take care of it—and they will take care of you, too, if you try to get it." I've played a lot of golf with Chandler as my partner, and those words stuck with him. Especially when you're young, starting out in golf, you're more susceptible to betting a little more then you should.

I recall the first time I met one young pro at the B.C. Open in Endicott, N.Y. "Hey, Mr. Snead," he said, "can I get a game with you? Can I play with you?"

"What's your name?" I said.

"Lon Hinkle."

"C'mon, let's go."

"Mr. Snead, I understand that you like to gamble a little bit."

"A little. What would you like to go for?"

He said a $5 nassau, so we went out and I beat him. He came into the locker room just grinning and laughing and gave me the $20.

The next time I saw him was at the Quad Cities Open, and he said, "Hey, Mr. Snead, I'd like to get my 20 back." So he lost again, grinning all the way around.

"Can he really afford this?" I asked a friend of his when we came in, and he said no.

So I said to him, "Lon, how about buying me a milk shake and forgetting the money?" I don't play the regular tour much anymore, and that's the last time I've played with Lon. But everytime I see him, he still reminds me of that milk shake he bought me and laughs about it.

The pros on tour like to play for a few dollars in practice rounds, but never once the tournament starts. It's silly to bet the other pro in your group when you're both playing for $100,000.

Fellows like Raymond Floyd and Lanny Wadkins will bet a little more than most in practice, but generally the going wager on tour is about $10. Take a guy like Jack Nicklaus, for instance, who has all the money in Florida. We've played a lot together and I don't ever remember playing him for any more than a couple of dollars.

The first time we met was in an exhibition in Ohio when Jack was about 16. He knew how good he was even then.

"Aren't you going to watch Snead give his clinic?" somebody asked him.

"No," he said, "I can beat him."

He was a little cocky back then, but he didn't beat me that day. The next week, though, he won the Ohio state open.

I played against Nicklaus years later in the Shell's Wonderful World of Golf series at Pebble Beach. We had a good match; it was close all the way. Then I missed a two-footer at the 10th that was all the difference. We came to the last hole even. I had my ball on the back of the green in three on the par 5 and almost chipped it in. Then Jack holed a great putt, at least 20 feet, for a birdie to beat me 1 up. We didn't have any money on the line that day, but Jack has never lacked for incentive.

I've not been what you call a big gambler on the golf course, although I have been around high rollers in my time. There used to be some high-stake matches played on Long Island, N.Y., in the 1930s that made my head spin. Those were the days when Walter Chrysler, the automotive baron, and Edward F. Hutton, the financier, would play $1,000 nassaus at the National Links in the morning and go to the races at Belmont in the afternoon. I didn't know either of those cats, but a fellow I did know who liked to play for money was T. Suffern (Tommy) Tailer, a pretty good Long Island amateur. I ran up against him in 1936 on the way to play in my first pro tournament at Shawnee-on-the-Delaware. Nobody knew me up there in that part of the country, so a friend arranged the match. Tailer said, "Who is this Sam Snead?" They said, "He just had his first train ride, came up from West Virginia, hayseed sticking out of his ears. But we'll back him for a $500 nassau, rain or shine."

We played the match at Meadow Brook on Long Island. I laid myself a stymie on the ninth hole and lost the front nine, but I beat him on the back nine and the 18. So my backers won $500 and I got a nice cut.

The next time we crossed paths was in 1938, when I received a call from Bunny Bacon, an average player who also played for high stakes. Bacon wanted me to play as his partner against Tailer and his partner, another high roller named Dr. Walter Hochschield. Apparently Tailer and Hochschield had issued Bacon a challenge in Palm Beach the previous winter: Bacon had to find himself a partner for a $5,000 match to be played at Meadow Brook; he needed to give them just 10 days notice and they would play. I think Tailer figured Bacon would grab some local pro, and Tommy knew he could handle anybody in New York.

Bacon offered me $300 plus expenses if we lost, $600 plus expenses if we won. I had just won the St. Paul Open, so Tailer didn't know I was within 800 miles of Meadow Brook. When he saw me on the putting green there on the day of the big match, he said, "Hello, Sam, what are you doing here?"

"I just came up to play a little," I said.

Well, you should have seen his face when I stepped on the first tee with Bacon. Bunny then said to Dr. Hochschield, "How about you and I playing a $2,000 individual on the side?" I don't know where he got the money, but Bacon was carrying 10 grand on his person. The doc took the bet, but he looked like rigor mortis had set in.

I was a little nervous myself with all those potatoes at stake, and I topped my drive and my second shot on the first hole. "What's going on here, Sam?" Bacon said, pulling me aside. "Tailer didn't get to you, did he?"

"Hell, no," I said, "nobody can fix me."

"I'm the one's that supposed to be shaking," he said.

I settled down after that and played pretty well. Tailer thought Hochschield would help him on three or four holes, but it ended up that he didn't help him a hole, nor did Bacon help me at all. They were playing each other, and both were off their games. I think Bunny won the fourth hole with a 14. You never saw such awful whacking and hacking in your life. But I had Tailer 4 down with four to play when he birdied 15 and 16, giving me some second thoughts. Then I eagled 17 to close out the match 3 and 1. Bunny beat Hochschield, too, collecting $7,000 altogether.

"I don't ever want to see you again," Tailer said.

Later he told Bacon that "Snead can't play." Every time I'd win a tournament, Bacon would say to Tailer, "Can't play, eh?"

I saw Tailer years later at the Cascades. Tommy Armour had got him to shorten his swing, and he was never any good after that. He used to have a big, fluid backswing and could knock the ball a mile. But now he had shortened his swing, he said, for more accuracy and lost all his distance. It just goes to show that you can shorten a long swing, but once it's shortened, you can never lengthen it again.

Just after that match at Meadow Brook, I got a call from L. B. Icely, the president of Wilson Sporting Goods Company, who wanted me to play a match in Cuba. It turned out that a well-known sportsman named Tommy Shevlin had gone on a drinking spree in New York with a Cuban millionaire named Thornwald Sanchez, and an argument developed. Sanchez said that his pro at the Havana Country Club, Rufino Gonzales, could beat anybody in the world at his home course.

"I know somebody who can beat him," said Shevlin.

"I got $5,000 that says he can't," said Sanchez.

Actually, Shevlin didn't have anybody in mind, so he called Mr. Icely for advice, and that's how I got the offer. I'd never been to Cuba before. When I arrived, everybody there had money on this match. What started as $5,000 must have grown at least to $100,000, which was a lot of pesos back in the '30s.

"How much do you want to bet?" Shevlin asked me.

"Nothing," I said. "This wasn't my idea. I've never seen this guy Gonzales before."

"Well, you've got $250 bet," he said. "It'll make us all feel better."

I played a practice round with Gonzales before the match and shot a 65. P. Hal Sims, the famous bridge expert and occasional golfer, was there and told me, "Don't play with him anymore. Don't show him what you've got." But after that one round, I knew where I could beat him. I had the edge on the par 5s, which I could reach in two and he couldn't, and on one par 4, where I could cut across the dogleg and knock it on.

But this Gonzales was no easy pigeon waiting to be plucked; he was very straight off the tee and a magician with the putter. When I got to the course on the day of the match, I saw all these rough-looking hombres around the first tee. It was then explained to me that they were Batista's boys, and that the dictator himself was betting on Gonzales. That's all I needed to hear; I already was jumpier than a cat burglar at the policeman's ball.

We played a 36-hole match, and it was decided on those long holes I figured. I shot 69-68 and Gonzales had 71-71. Batista's boys pressed in pretty close to us as we walked back to the clubhouse, so I wasted no time collecting my winnings and hightailing it out of the country. "Good luck," I said to Gonzales, who had to face the hometown fans.

Back in Miami, the first person I ran into was Mr. Icely.

"You feeling all right, Sam?" he asked.

"Next time the stakes are that high, send Demaret, will you?" I said. "He likes to travel and would make a prettier corpse than me."

4

How to Read Your Opponents

My old partner in the sporting goods business, Ted Williams, used to tell me how he studied pitchers on the mound. He said he watched every move they made—the look in their eyes, the twitching of their fingers, the shifting of their feet—and he waited for a pattern. Eventually Williams could read the pitch before it left the pitcher's hand. When a blooper was coming, he knew it and knocked the ball out of the park.

I always tried to be just as observant on the golf course. I watched the guys on tour so closely that I could walk around the locker room and tell you whose shoes belonged to whom, just by the way they were worn down. I could pick Art Wall's shoes, for instance, out of a million pairs. Art has funny feet—a very high instep, with his toes turned up a bit. There was a time when you could cover over any tour player from the knees up and I could name him by his walk.

"So what?" you say. Well, knowing players' mannerisms helps you learn where their weaknesses are. Most fellows have a pattern to the way they play golf. When the screws get tighter on the closing holes of a match, watch for their mannerisms to change. Bobby Jones always said that he paid attention to his opponent's feet; if a player widened his stance toward the end of a round, Jones knew he was tiring and it was only a matter of time for his opponent to make a mistake.

When an opponent breaks his pattern, you have the edge. And the funny thing is, once you've got a person's number, it seems like you can beat him every time. Jimmy Demaret beat me for the Match Play Championship in San Francisco in 1938, but after that I never lost a match to him. Whenever he'd say, "Hurry up, let's get this over with," I knew he'd already beaten himself. But usually the signs are not so obvious.

Another year in that San Francisco match play tournament, I was playing Ben Hogan with the match all even going down the 17th fairway. All of a sudden I noticed that Ben was talking with the gallery, which is something he just never did. "Ben, ol' boy, I've got you today," I said to myself. Almost on cue, Hogan missed the 18th green and I won with a par. It wasn't so much that Ben fell apart; seeing him break his pattern gave me a tremendous boost of confidence, and I think that was the difference.

The man who taught me to study my opponents was Freddie Martin, who used to be the manager at the Greenbrier Hotel at White Sulphur Springs, W.Va. "You know, Sam, man is still a primitive being," Freddie said. "Let someone betray a weakness and instinctively he's ready for the kill."

I'll always remember the story he told me about the famous playoff for the 1913 U.S. Open, when an unknown American amateur named Francis Ouimet beat the British giants, Harry Vardon and Ted Ray. According to Freddie, Vardon never smoked on the course, but on the 13th hole, a stroke behind the upstart Ouimet, Vardon took out a cigarette. Ouimet noticed Harry's hands shaking when he tried to light up. "I shouldn't have to tell you what it did for Ouimet's courage," said Freddie. "It went up like the price of bum whisky. He birdied No. 17 after Vardon hooked into a dogleg bunker, took a 3 to Vardon's 5, and won the National Open."

The first opportunity I had to use this ploy in a big tournament was the 1942 PGA, at Seaview Country Club in Atlantic City, N.J. I played Jim Turnesa in the 36-hole final, and we were dead even after 27 holes.

It happened on the 10th tee, our 28th hole of the day. There was no change in Jim's brisk walk or confident demeanor, but as he stood over his tee shot he changed his waggle—that little back-and-forth movement of the clubhead just prior to the takeaway. All day Jim had waggled twice before pulling the trigger. But now the waggles were not as smooth as before. They were short and jerky. And there were four waggles instead of two. Something was wrong, and I knew it.

Turnesa hooked his ball into the trees in the left rough, hit another tree coming out and I won the hole with a 4. It was a turning point in the match. Jim then three-putted the 30th hole, and I beat him 2 and 1 to win my first major championship.

Another subtle change in mannerisms helped me win the 1954 Masters Tournament and again it involved Ben Hogan. He and I tied after 72 holes, and in those days (before sudden-death playoffs) ties were broken by an 18-hole round on Monday. A business associate of mine, Gary Nixon, came to Augusta that year trying to get a wager on me in the playoff but he couldn't find any takers. I told him he was probably lucky, because Hogan was playing awfully well.

We matched each other shot for shot on the front nine, with 35s apiece. I chipped in from 65 feet on the 10th to go one ahead. Then I bogeyed 12 to square the match. On No. 13, the reachable par 5, I carried a big drive around the dogleg, hit a 3-iron on the green and two-putted for a birdie to go one stroke ahead again (Hogan laid up and made a par). Ben and I each went par-birdie on the next two holes, so I still led by one going into the par-3 16th. I hit it in there about 25 feet away and Ben hit it inside me, 18 feet away. Just for a moment I noticed an uneasiness in the way he was looking over his putt—a hesitation—and I decided to give mine a bold roll. It had been raining so the green was slower than normal. I gave it a hard rap and the ball stopped about a foot past the hole. Then Ben made a short jabbing stroke that hit the ground behind the ball and left himself five feet short. This was not the same Hogan who had played 15 flawless holes that day. He missed that second putt, giving me a two-stroke lead. I ran into trouble on the 17th hole when my drive came to rest in a divot hole, but I felt relaxed because of what I had seen on the previous green. I swung down hard on a 6-iron, the ball took off perfectly and stopped 40 feet from the hole. Both of us made pars. Then on No. 18, I hit my approach into the front bunker, but still feeling at ease I blasted out and two-putted from four feet to win my third Masters, 70 to 71. I really believe that Ben's little hesitation on the 16th hole gave me the psychological advantage.

People say, "Play the course; don't play the man," but I never believed that. Especially in match play, you have to keep one eye on your opponent. And as Freddie Martin used to say, when you notice a weakness, go for the kill.

- I recommend that you study the habits of the people you play with. Pay close attention to their eyes, because fear often shows up as an enlargement of the pupils. My motto is, big pupils lead to big scores.
- Take a look at your opponent's lips on the first tee, and keep checking them throughout the round. If a white rash shows around his lips, he's probably got the heebie-jeebies—double the wager.
- Watch for temper tantrums. An angry golfer is a loser; if he can't control himself, he can't control his shots. Tommy Bolt used to turn red when he got mad. It started at the back of his neck; when it reached the tips of his ears, watch out—the clubs would start flying. He didn't care anymore and he lost his concentration. You could stick a fork in him; he was done.
- Look for changes in your opponent's putting style. If he's choking, that's where the twitches show up first.
- Watch for indecision. If a player can't make up his mind, mistakes are sure to follow. The one exception to this rule was Cary Middlecoff. He's the only man I ever saw who could get set over a shot and change his club four times and then pick the club he had the first time and hit a perfect shot. But aside from Cary, show me a fellow who keeps switching clubs and I'll press the bet every time.
- Study the natural rhythm of his stride. If a fast-walker suddenly slows down, or if a dawdler speeds up, it means he's on the ropes.

Of course, reading your opponent doesn't always work out according to plan. I remember being paired with Dan Sikes in the last round of the Doral Open in 1963. Dan had to make a 10-footer at 15, a five-footer at 16 and a seven-footer at 17—all for pars—to stay one stroke ahead of me. Walking up to the 18th tee, I could hear him huffing and puffing like a runner in the Boston Marathon. "I got him now," I thought.

Sure enough, he pushed his drive into a fairway bunker and then played a 3-iron to about 90 feet from the hole. I hit my drive down the middle and then a 3-iron 12 feet away. Sikes rolled his first putt to five feet, huffing and puffing all the way. I could see him crumbling, so I didn't want to do anything foolish like three-putt. I tapped mine up for a gimme and watched as Dan, still out of breath, drained the winning putt. So much for telltale signs in that tournament. But believe me, reading your opponent darn near always works.

5

How to Spot A Hustler

"Son, no matter how far you travel, or how smart you get, always remember this: Some day, somewhere, a guy is going to come to you and show you a nice brand-new deck of cards on which the seal is never broken, and this guy is going to offer to bet you that the jack of spades will jump out of this deck and squirt cider in your ear. But, son, do not bet him, for as soon as you do you are going to get an ear full of cider."

—Damon Runyon

A good bettor is suspicious by nature. He doesn't trust his own kinfolk when it comes to a dollar wager. If somebody offers you a sucker bet, think twice because you might be the sucker.

I always said, you should never gamble with a stranger, and consider everyone a stranger until you've played with him at least a dozen times. You can go broke judging a book by its cover; a lot of golfers have.

I remember back in the summer of 1934 I met a couple of hustlers who later became tour winners, Dutch Harrison and Bob Hamilton. They had been playing 50-cent skins with two school teachers on vacation in Pinehurst, N.C. (A skin is won when a player has the lowest score on a hole; if two or more tie for low, then all tie.) When their fish ran out of half-dollars, Bob spotted me sitting on a split-rail fence by the first tee. He didn't know who I was, and I probably wasn't an imposing figure back in those days, fresh out of the Virginia mountains. "Don't look now," Bob said to Dutch, "but I think we got ourselves a replacement."

"Say, fella, would you like to play a little game of 50-cent skins?" Dutch asked me.

"Sounds good, but how much can I lose?" I said, checking my pockets. They figured I had enough, and off we went.

Dutch later told me that their hearts sunk when I put my hands on the club and cranked up my big swing. Back in those days my swing looked prettier than a red heifer in a flower bed. I won 12 skins in 18 holes; Bob and Dutch had none. After the round, Dutch took me aside and said that Pinehurst was a big resort with more than one 18-hole course; they'd appreciate it if I picked one and stayed off their turf.

Titanic Thompson, the well-known gambler, used to make all sorts of bets that the victim thought he couldn't lose. He bet a fellow once that he could throw a pecan over a three-story clubhouse. Of course, he neglected to say the pecan was full of buckshot. He'd bet that he could guess the total weight of a half-dozen waitresses in a restaurant (he put them on a scale the day before). He'd bet that of the next 30 persons who would walk into a bar, at least two would have the same birthday, which seems like a losing proposition, but actually the odds are even money after 20 persons. His philosophy was, if you're not a world champion golfer learn to be a world champion at something, so you can double up and get your money back.

Even when you're on your guard, you sometimes can't avoid getting hoodwinked. I figure I get hustled at least a couple of times a year. Three guys came down to the Greenbrier one year—a 10, a 12 and a 14. The low handicapper was dressed in brown pants, a gray shirt, a red hat, white socks and the ugliest pair of shoes you've ever seen that hadn't been polished since the day he bought them. He looked like four steps below a Mafia don. I said, "My fee is $100 plus caddie."

"We don't want no lesson," the chief said. "We just want to play for a little something."

"What do you want to play for?" I said.

"Whatever you want."

I knew that was a bad sign, but I didn't have anything better to do. The 14-handicapper was inside me on the first five holes! At that point, I said, "Fellas, just let me get home with my golf clubs." I ended up shooting 65 and losing. If I had shot 70, they would have owned the hotel.

Another time three of us were playing in Boca Raton, when a guy comes running up to the 10th tee. "Mr. Snead, I'd like to play the last nine holes with you. Give me a shot on everything but the par 3s. I'll play you for either $10 a hole or a straight $25."

I bet him $25, and he shot 35 on the back nine with a 7 on one hole, for a net 28. Naturally he won. When I came in, a member said to me, "Don't you know that guy?"

"No, I never saw him before," I said.

"He clipped Arnold for $300 the other day."

Two years later I saw this guy again at the Greenbrier, but he didn't think I recognized him. He came over to me with another fellow and said, "How about a little game tomorrow?"

"Sure," I said. "What's your handicap?"

"Mine is 12 and he's a 14," he said pointing to his friend.

"By the way, where do you play mostly?"

This caught him unawares, and he said "Inwood." So I called Inwood Country Club in New York, where I knew Ellsworth Vines was the pro. I figured it was worth the $5 telephone bill to get the goods on these birds. "The young one is a 3-handicap and the other guy is an 8, but the 3 can play closer to it than the 8," said Vines.

So the next morning I grabbed these guys at breakfast and said: "You're not a 12 and he's not a 14. You didn't think I remembered your hustling me at Boca, did you? I called your club to check your handicaps. You're a 3 and he's an 8. I'll play you dudes today, but all you're getting is your handicap."

Now I was at least a plus-4 at the Greenbrier, meaning my handicap was four strokes on the other side of scratch, so I had a big edge (though it was deserved). I shot 64 and beat them both. Afterward I said, "You boys are going to get hurt if you keep up this hustling. If I wasn't the pro here, I'd have taken a swipe at you myself. I want you out of here right away, and don't ever come back to the Greenbrier again."

When you find yourself caught in the middle of a hustle, your best bet is to cut your losses and go quietly. Bing Crosby once got taken by a legendary golf bettor from California called the Mysterious John Montague. Montague bet that he could beat Crosby in an 18-hole match using only a baseball bat, a shovel and a rake while Bing was allowed to use his full set of clubs. On the par-5 first hole, Montague hit two fungoes that put him in a greenside bunker, shoveled out and raked the putt in for a birdie 4. Crosby took a $100 bill out of his wallet, handed it to Montague and walked back to the clubhouse.

I figure that the first time you get hustled it's his fault; the second time it's your own fault.

How do you head off a hustle?

Rule 1: Bet with strangers only after they've become friends.

Rule 2: Try to check your opponent's left hand. If there's a noticeable callus running across the base of the ring and little fingers, think again.

Rule 3: Beware of anyone with a suntan darker than your own.

Rule 4: Keep your betting simple. Don't allow an opponent to distract you with multiple side wagers or confusing gimmick bets.

Rule 5: Check your opponent's handicap. If you both belong to the same club, take a minute on your way out of the locker room to inspect his latest handicap. If you're playing someone from another club and the wager is sizable, invest in a phone call.

Rule 6: Bet with your head, not your ego. Someone probably will have the edge going off the first tee. Make sure it's not the other guy.

Rule 7: Never bet a sick man. An opponent who's hurting doesn't have room in his mind for anything but his golf game. I shot a course-record 64 at the Cascades one day when I was so hoarse I couldn't talk. Somebody asked me what I'd have shot if I felt good and I said 71 or 72.

Rule 8: Don't play against an unemployed golfer. Either he doesn't have any money or he practices all day. You can't win either way.

Rule 9: Never play a golfer with a 1-iron in his bag, especially if his handicap is in double figures.

Rule 10: Run—do not walk—away from an opponent who asks for fewer strokes than he's been getting and at the same time wants to increase the bet. This is the oldest hustler's ploy in the book. A golfer tried to pull it on me once years ago. He said he was a low-80s shooter, so I gave him 14 strokes—or a shot a hole on everything but the 3s—and we played a $10 nassau. I shot four straight rounds between 66 and 68, but we broke exactly even each time.

Then one morning he said, "I feel hot today. Let's play $250 a side, and you can give me 12 strokes instead of 14."

"Thanks, but I'll pass," I said. Later I learned that he really was a scratch player, capable of shooting in the low 70s. He'd just come from Hollywood where he hustled one of the movie stars out of $100,000.

6

How to Accommodate a Pigeon

S how me a man with a fast backswing and a thick wallet, and I'll go get my golf clubs. I don't exactly set out to hunt for pigeons, but when one presents himself on my doorstep, Ol' Sam will accommodate him.

Nick the Greek Dandolos used to say: "The next best thing to playing and winning is playing and losing. The main thing is to play." Well, that's the kind of golfer I want to bet—somebody more interested in playing than winning.

Patience is the key to getting the right match. You have to be willing to turn down proposal after proposal until your opponent, who's less patient, makes you an offer you can't refuse. Sometimes you won't play at all on a particular day, or maybe you'll go out without a match. Consider it an investment. You've called your opponent's bluff, and now he knows that when you say you won't take a match, that's what you mean.

The real pigeon is a golfer who loves to play so much that he has to play; he will take the short side of a match just because he wants the action. Call him the Happy Loser.

Another type of pigeon I like to play is the Bantam Rooster. He's the fellow at your course who struts around the clubhouse porch telling everybody how good he is, how he reached 18 with a drive and a wedge, how he's playing better than ever. Remember, it's the rooster who crows; the hen lays the egg. Normally this type is a good player, but his handicap is about two strokes lower than it should be. His ego won't allow him to take strokes from anyone, and with a little coaxing he'll give you one or two more than the difference between your handicaps. There's a saying: "He couldn't play to it, but he could pay to it." Just keep telling the Bantam Rooster how far he's hitting the ball; you're only beating him because your putts are dropping and his aren't. The funny thing about this fellow is that he never learns; he just goes on thinking that he's the victim of bad luck. As they say in the hills, "Man is the only bird that can be plucked more than once."

The third type of pigeon is the Nervous Nellie. He likes to play for a little money, but he falls apart when the stakes go up. In poker, if somebody raises above the level of comfort, you can always fold a weak hand. In golf, when the press bets get heavy, you just can't quit; you're stuck out there in the middle of the course and you have to play your way to the clubhouse. That's when the Nervous Nellies can lose a bundle. If you can get your opponent to play for a few dollars more than his comfort level—as long as you can afford it!—you have the edge.

And rounding out my foursome of easy marks is the Hurry-Up-And-Hit Harry. He's the guy who is always late getting to the first tee. He comes running up, out of breath, with a hamburger in one hand, trying to tie his golf shoes with the other. This fellow's mind is back at the office, and he's ripe for the plucking. I've always remembered something I heard about Henry Cotton, who insisted on having somebody else drive him to the course in his own maroon Mercedes, preferably his opponent, because he didn't want to get unnerved. Another tip that stuck with me was something Ben Hogan told his partner, Jimmy Demaret, at the Inverness Four-Ball. One day when they had a late starting time, Jimmy announced he was going to play gin rummy before the round.

"No, you're not, Jimmy," said Hogan. "When you play cards you get all tensed up waiting for a card to come. That's the worst thing you can do before playing golf."

Walter Hagen used to do everything in slow motion on the morning of a big match, including shaving and combing his hair. Watch for the guy in a hurry; he can't wait to give you his money.

Getting back to that guy with a fast backswing and a thick wallet, I remember once playing a heavyset Cuban named Tomeu who fit that description and had all the money in Havana. I beat him for *mucho dinero* one summer, but he wouldn't be discouraged. I kept giving him more strokes and he kept raising the wagers. I had to open up a new bank account; he'd filled one up. I was giving him a stroke a hole, and he still couldn't win.

"Let's forget it," I told him. "Why don't you go back home to your cattle ranch?" Which was the wrong thing to say because he had a little of the Bantam Rooster in him.

"No, hunting season on," he said. "I beat you yet."

The next day I gave him a stroke a hole on the par 3s and 4s and two strokes on the par 5s. Tomeu still lost. Then I gave him two strokes on every hole more than 400 yards and one stroke everywhere else. He lost even more.

"I give up," I told him.

"No, you don't," he said. "Hunting season still on."

Then I played him using only one club, a 3-wood, for all shots, including putts. He used all 14 clubs and we played even. I shot 78 and buried him.

"How's the hunting season?" I asked.

"What you give me now?" he said, ignoring my wisecrack.

I was running out of ideas when it occurred to me that I learned to play golf as a kid swinging a swamp maple that I had carved into the shape of a golf club. "I'll give you one last bet," I told Tomeu. "I'll play you with a stick and a wedge and nothing else, OK?"

"Let me see stick?" he said.

I went out into the woods, found a swamp maple about 45 inches long and started my whittling. After a couple of days I had it shaped the way I wanted and then showed it to Tomeu.

"Hunting season back on," he said.

We went out and played a match before a large hometown gallery, everybody thinking I'd gone crazy. But I just slowed down my tempo, made my normal big swing and knocked the ball out of sight. I used the swamp maple off the tee and on long fairway shots, and I chipped and putted with the wedge. I shot a swamp-maple record 76, which sent Tomeu home on the next steamer.

"Goddamn hunting season closed for good," he said.

7

Getting Off the First Tee With an Edge

There's a song that goes, "There are 50 ways to leave your lover," but take it from Sam Snead: there are only two ways to leave the first tee—with you having the edge or with your opponent having the edge. There's no such thing as a dead-even match. So I always figured if somebody's got to have an advantage, it might as well be Ol' Sam.

Besides, the ideal betting proposition is not an even match between two sides; the ideal bet occurs when both sides think they have the edge because then the stakes tend to be high. Of course, you want to be on the side that really does have it. Titanic Thompson, golf's greatest hustler, used to say, "To be a winner, a man has to feel good about himself and know he has some kind of skillful advantage going in." It's amazing how that little bit of inside information helps you play better.

I got hooked up once in a match with Leonard Dodson, who was a pretty good player and gambler back in the '40s. We were in Kansas City, and Leonard met a couple of amateurs in a bar who had high opinions of their golf games. They wanted to challenge Leonard and his partner, me, to a $1,000 nassau. I was ready to leave town for the next tour stop, but Leonard talked me into playing the match.

"Who are these guys? They must be good to bet $1,000," I said to Dodson.

"I don't care who they are," he said. "You're bleeping Sam Snead, and I'm no piker. We can take 'em."

We did pluck those guys for a bundle as it turned out, but caution never hurt anybody—especially when it comes to a wager. I've always been accused of being conservative in my match making and I plead guilty. There's no sense going off the first tee all even when you can start 1 or 2 up.

I've been on the receiving end of this philosophy a few times in my day. At Vero Beach in Florida one winter, I ran up against a guy with a 14-handicap who shot 68 on his own ball, and his partner helped him two strokes, for a 52 net better ball. How are you going to beat that? I believe in a comfortable advantage, but that was a little too comfortable.

I used to spend some time at a municipal course where the assistant pro was named Bill. "I'll put the bag on somebody," I used to say when I'd get there in the morning. And by the end of the day, I'd have me a sweet match.

"You'll never put the bag on me," Bill used to say, but I kept bugging him for a match. He was built like a guy who was meant to be big, but his arms and legs were cut short. He was only about 5-4, but sitting down he looked a foot taller.

One day it was raining and the course was closed. "C'mon, Bill, let's go play," I said.

"No, I'm busy," he said, but finally gave in. They opened the course for us, and we had a little gallery.

"All right, you SOB," he said to me on the first tee, "you're going to give me five strokes a side."

Well, he had no trouble breaking 80, so I knew it was a tough bet. (Of course, I was about a plus-6 at the time, meaning my handicap was six strokes better than the course rating.) I was averaging 66 around that track, so I figured I'd give it a shot.

After eight holes I was 1 up. On the ninth hole, he made a 20-footer for a birdie and I had about a 15-footer to halve him on the hole and win the front nine. He tiptoed up to the hole to take out his ball, acting as if he'd just won the National Open. While his hand was still in the hole, I hit my putt. Just as he straightened up, bang, my ball went in for another birdie! He jumped about three feet.

On the back nine, we were all even after 17 holes. The 18th is a par 5 where Bill was getting a stroke. I hit a good drive and knocked my second shot in there 12 to 14 feet from the hole. He made his 5 for a net 4, figuring he had tied the match. Then I made my curler for an eagle to win.

"SOB, I knew you were going to beat me," he said.

"I'll tell you what I'll do," I said, offering him a chance to get his money back. "I'll let you put your drive where mine finishes and still give you five strokes a side."

"No way," he said, "you'll just drive into the rough, and you know I can't hit it out of there."

Bill was no dummy, so that match never came off.

One thing you never, repeat never, do is downgrade your opponent. I don't care if he can't hit the broad side of a barn with a snow shovel, you've got to believe—and say—he's just down on his luck. You always want to overestimate your opponent's abilities and underestimate your own. Give a wide berth to the fellow who's always telling you how good you're playing. You've got to have a little John Barrymore in you to make a guy think he's just put the bite on you when actually all he's got in his mouth is the bait. The whole idea is to relieve a golfer of his bankroll and make him love it. It's not as hard to do as you might think. But, remember, you must leave him with his self-respect. Never gloat over a victory. You were just lucky and he couldn't make a putt.

SETTING THE TRAP: Your first move in arranging a match is to ask your opponent what his handicap is. No matter the answer, express astonishment at its liberality. Surely the handicap committee has erred. Is he turning in all his scores?

What you want to stress is that all you're looking for is a decent match, one that's fair. Playing 100 percent of the difference in your handicaps would be ridiculous; he's too good a player for that. You might even want to make a trip to the locker room to scrutinize the handicap sheet. Once you've established that a victory by you would be a miracle on the order of Lourdes, you're ready to move on to deciding the exact handicap.

AGREEING ON THE HANDICAP: One of the rules I like to play by is that the higher handicapper in match play gets only three-quarters of the difference between his handicap and his opponent's. Naturally, I'm usually the lower handicapper and this works to my advantage, but I think it's only fair. Handicaps are established for stroke-play competition, not match play. The high handicapper knows he's going to have a few 6s and 7s, but they're more than offset with his net birdies. So if you're the low handicapper, I'd urge you to make a strong case for three-quarters of the handicap difference. If your opponent won't go for it, offer to play him at stroke play, matching your total scores. If you're the high handicapper, insist on match play—and take 100 percent of the handicap difference, if you can get it.

Options to consider in close matches are half-strokes and safety holes. If you and your opponent are roughly even, start by asking for one or two strokes handicap. Then as a compromise, offer to accept a half-stroke, which means if you tie you win (by a half-stroke). If that doesn't work, settle for a safety hole, which means if you lose 1 down you can use the safety to tie. You can tie with a safety, but you can't win with it. Most important, whatever terms you arrive at for the match, take a moment to write them down on the back of the scorecard and repeat them to your opponent. It could save an argument after the round.

One decision that should not be overlooked is where the handicap strokes fall. There are two possibilities: playing off scratch or playing off the low handicapper in the group.

If you're playing off scratch, everybody gets his full handicap: a 6-handicapper gets six strokes and an 18-handicapper gets 18. If you're playing off the low handicapper and he, for example, is a 6, he gets no strokes and the 18-handicapper gets 12. What's the difference? Well, it could decide the match.

"The key is figuring out where the shots fall on the card," says Dr. Cary Middlecoff, who's made a study of it in his matches back home at the Memphis Country Club. "If I'm the low man and I have to give a lot of strokes on the par 5s that I can't reach in two or birdie easily, then I'm going to yell and scream to make sure I get all my strokes. But if I've got a partner who can help me out on those holes, I'll opt for playing off my ball. You've got to study where the strokes come and figure how best to protect yourself."

8

When to Press the Bet

My old friend Bobby Riggs, the tennis hustler, was a master of the press bet in golf. A "press" is an additional wager usually equal to the original bet that starts when it's announced and runs through the remaining holes to be played on that nine. For example, if you're playing the front nine for $2 and you're 2 down after the sixth hole, you can press for another $2, which means that the original wager continues and the second bet applies to the seventh, eighth and ninth holes. If you win the three remaining holes, you win the original bet 1 up for $2 plus you win the press 3 up for another $2.

I remember when Riggs divorced his second wife, Priscilla, and left their home in Golden Beach, Fla., he was more broken up about losing his neighbor George Morton Levy as a golf partner. George was a harness racing entrepreneur who consistently shot his age. They were a formidable pair on the golf course. Bobby always had the edge going into a match so it was only a matter of time before their opponents wanted to press the bet. Bobby then would consult with his partner, and George would shake his head and pace back and forth on the tee looking worried.

"Robert, you know I don't enjoy playing for that kind of money," he would scold Riggs, then ever so reluctantly agree to the press. Riggs and Levy won a lot of money with this routine.

The ground rules for press bets should be made clear on the first tee. The player who is down in the match has the option to press. If you're ahead, you cannot press unless your opponent suggests it. Most bettors play that you must be 2 down to press; they don't accept 1-down presses. But a common wager is the "end press," which is an automatic press bet on the last hole, the ninth or 18th. You also can play automatic 2-down presses, which means that whenever either side goes 2 down, a new press bet starts. For instance, Sam and Ben are playing a $5 nassau. Sam loses the first two holes—automatic press—and wins the next two holes. Sam is even on the original bet and 2 up on the press, which automatically starts another press. Say, Ben wins the next two holes. Sam is 2 down on the original, even on the first press and 2 down on the second press. Of course, Sam wins the remaining three holes. How does the match stand? He wins the original 1 up, the first press 3 up, the second press 1-up, the third press 3 up and the fourth press 1 up. Sam collects $25.

Unless you're playing automatic presses, both parties have to agree on the press. Not all golfers realize this. A lot of people think you have to accept a press. While some may say it's unsportsmanlike to decline a press, your money is at stake and you can pass or play as you see fit.

I know some golfers who get down in a match and keep pressing. They figure it's like flipping a coin; if you keep doubling the bet, heads is bound to come up eventually. But a lot of times, tails keeps coming up and they either run out of money or, in golf, run out of holes.

Another type of golfer tries to be cagey with his press bets. He'll wait until he gets to a stroke hole before pressing. Don't be afraid to turn down the bet. I tell my opponents, "You either press when you're 2 down or you don't get a press from me."

The best way to eliminate all arguments is to play automatic 2-down presses. But let me add two cautionary notes: (1) Make sure you have the edge going in, because these presses can multiply in a hurry, and (2) make sure you have enough money to cover the worst case, losing every hole, because you want to be able to play the match with a clear mind. If your opponent doesn't want to play automatic presses, at least get him to agree on two points: the press must be made by the losing side immediately upon becoming 2 down, and both sides must agree on the press. My rule of thumb on when to press is pretty simple. If I'm playing well and/or I have a substantial edge in the match (60-40 is the breaking point), I press. If I'm not hitting it pure and/or the bounces seem to be going the other fellow's way, you won't hear a peep out of me.

It's amazing how bets can pyramid and you can lose the cardigan off your back because of these presses. If you start out playing a straight three-way $2 nassau with automatic 2-down presses on each nine and end presses on nine and 18, how much do you think you can lose on a bad day? Say, you're beaten 5 down on both sides, including losses on the ninth and 18th holes. That would mean you lose four presses and the original bet on each nine, plus the 18-hole bet, which adds up to $22. If you have two individual matches and one team match, you could lose $60 or more playing $2 nassaus.

Like most good hustlers, Bobby Riggs asks his opponent for a press nonchalantly, the way you would ask a passerby on the street for the time of day. He makes money sound insignificant, as if it's an insult even to talk about it. "I'll give you a press," he says quickly in a hushed tone, as if the proposal is as natural as the sun rising in the morning. Of course he'll give you the press. Of course you'll accept it.

In 1953 at the Greenbrier in White Sulphur Springs, W.Va., where I used to be the pro, Bobby Riggs got tangled up in a match with an oil tycoon from Evansville, Ind., named Ray Ryan. Bobby could shoot in the low 80s when he wanted to, lower when the bet was right, and he had to give this fellow a stroke on all the holes but the par 3s. Ryan was a protege of George Low, but Low wasn't around to coach him this week. They started out playing a $1,000 nassau. Every time the oilman got 2 down, he pressed for another grand. Bobby won $10,000 the first day. Then they raised the stakes, the oilman got a stroke on every hole including the par 3s, and Bobby won $20,000 the second day. By the end of the week, with all those presses, Riggs had taken the old boy for $180,000, which stands till this day as the biggest haul ever made in a golf match at the Greenbrier.

9

How to Outwit
Your Opponent

I'll never forget the time I was in the Boston Red Sox dugout with my old business partner Ted Williams. They were about to play the Yankees, and Ted and I got into a discussion about "the power hand" in baseball and golf. Ted was a left-hander, of course. He claimed that his power hand was his right. I said, "No, you lead the bat in with the right and you whack it over with your left, just like I do in golf. I'm right-handed so I lead the club down with my left and then, once I get in position, I whack it with my right."

Ted went 0 for 4 that day. "You and your goddamn power hand," he fumed after the game. All he could think of at the plate was which hand to whack it with.

That reminds me of a tournament I played in West Virginia back in 1935, before I ever knew what the word "gamesmanship" meant. I was leading by three shots going into the last round and paired with my boss, Freddie Glein, who was a little jealous of my success. Back in those days I drove the ball with a 3-wood I'd made myself from a block of wood. It didn't have an insert, but I covered the face with carpet tacks. You never heard such a cracking sound as when I connected with that 3-wood, and I was hitting it long and straight.

"Sam, what did you do to your swing?" Freddie asked me on the first tee. "You're finishing with your elbow real high. It's flipping all around on your follow-through."

I guess I was finishing a little like Arnold Palmer does, with a blocking motion that keeps the ball from hooking. But after Freddie's tip, I concentrated on keeping my left elbow down, and I started hitting left-to-left shots—they started left and then hooked farther left. I needed a huntin' dog to find my tee shots. Even when I tried to forget what Freddie told me, I couldn't keep the ball in play. I shot 80 and threw away the tournament.

There's a famous story that some people say happened to Frank Stranahan and others say it was Lawson Little. I'm not sure who was the original victim, but it's been pulled on a lot of golfers since. The poor guy was playing well when a fan came up to him after one round and said, "Excuse me, sir. May I ask you a question? I've always wondered, do you inhale or exhale when you hit the ball?" It sounded like an innocent question, and the unsuspecting golfer thought awhile and replied he wasn't really sure. It got him thinking, though, and for a golfer who's playing well overthinking can be disastrous. On every swing the next day he was trying to decide if he breathed in or out at impact. He started hitting the ball all over the course. He was really hot after the round. Then he spotted the fellow who asked him the question standing in the parking lot. "Look, mister," he said, "you've cost me the tournament with your stupid question. If you ever learn how to breathe, I hope you forget."

Gamesmanship is trying to beat a player with your mouth instead of your golf clubs. I never went in for it much, but if somebody pulled a bit of gamesmanship on me I didn't hesitate to reply in kind. I remember once a young rookie on tour started kidding me about my sidesaddle putting. "Son," I told him, "don't fool with me. I've got a needle longer than your leg, and it's got a hook on the end of it." Another time I was playing a match against George Bayer in the Shell's Wonderful World of Golf series when he started pulling the funny business. I birdied the first two holes to go 2 up, and walking to the third tee, Big George throws me the needle. I stopped him right in his tracks. "Listen, George," I said, "you beat me with your clubs, not your mouth." That was the end of it, and we didn't have any problems from there in. You have to be firm with gamesmen; you can't let them get away with anything or pretty soon they own you.

The fellows who get on my nerves are the ones that pull the Magnet Act on you. They plant a negative thought in your mind about a hazard on the course and your ball goes to it like a magnet. I was playing in Charleston, W.Va., once when my opponent says on one tee, "Now be careful, Sam, there's trouble over there on the right. You want to stay away from that creek on the right side." Don't you know that's where I hit my ball. I gave him some of his own treatment on the next tee and then we called a truce.

I prefer to play with golfers who don't talk much on the course; we don't get in each other's way. The best fellow for that was my old rival, Ben Hogan. No one ever could accuse him of gamesmanship. Ben always played in silence. I remember when we played off the 1954 Masters, we shook hands on the first tee and wished each other luck. I knew both of us were lying. Then we didn't say another word the rest of the round. Maybe Ben said, "You're away," a couple of times, but we didn't have a conversation. Some people might think that the silent treatment is a form of gamesmanship, but we just wanted to let our clubs do the talking. By the way, I beat him that day, 70 to 71.

The worst case of gamesmanship I've ever been a victim of happened in the Rochester (N.Y.) Open. I was leading the tournament, playing in the last group with Lloyd Mangrum and Clayton Heafner. On the seventh hole, Lloyd missed the green and chipped about 12 feet past the hole. Without bothering to mark his ball, he stood off to the side leaving his ball on the green. I looked my putt over from a couple of angles and then addressed the ball. Just as I got ready to hit it, he walked across my line and marks his ball. I backed off and started over, but it broke my concentration. I didn't come close to making the putt. On the ninth tee, he stood no more than four feet from where I had my ball teed; then just as I began to forward press, he crossed his feet. I stood back and said, "Lloyd, I'm giving you and Clayton every opportunity to play. Don't bother me. That's all I'm asking. Now get the hell off the tee until I shoot." At this point a guy in the gallery hollers, "Attaboy, Sam, he's been doing it to you on every hole." Neither Mangrum nor Heafner said a word to me. I was playing with a couple of dead fish. When I got four or five shots ahead and they realized they couldn't catch me, they started joking and kidding with one another. Whenever I hit a shot I always looked to see where they were, but there were no shenanigans the rest of the round.

Gamesmanship happens at all levels of the game. Let me give you two examples—one in a $5 nassau and the other in the U.S. Open. Back when I was 60 years old and trying to break my age for the first time, I had two putts from 30 feet for a 59 on the last hole at the Old White Course at the Greenbrier. The fellow I was playing for a fin stood about seven presses down, and he probably was going to lose the last hole, too. As I was getting ready to putt, he started hitting his shoe with his putter and said, "You are going to three-putt, you are going to three-putt."

"George, get the hell away from me," I said. "I can two-putt for a 59, one-putt for a 58. Now I want to see if...."

"No, you're going to three-putt, three-putt," he said.

He really got my nanny. I left the first putt three feet short and missed the second. I could have killed him.

You may be aware of this second example. I've become more famous for losing the U.S. Open than for any tournament I've ever won. In the 1947 U.S. Open at St. Louis Country Club, Lew Worsham and I tied for the championship and had an 18-hole playoff. Lew and I were friends long before that Open and, of course, long afterward, but we played one tough match.

I wasn't playing very well, but I still stood two strokes ahead of Worsham going into the 16th hole. He made a long birdie putt there and I missed mine, so the margin was cut to one. On the 17th hole, my 8-iron approach shot ran just over the back of the green into the collar of rough that was matted down where people had been standing. I had to play a tricky little chip against the rough grain. Lew was so nervous he was out of breath. As I got over my ball, I could hear him wheezing like he'd just run the 100-yard dash. "Hey, could you back up a bit and give me a little breathing room?" I said. He did, and I hit a shot that came out a little fluffy and left me about six feet short, which I missed. That put us even.

On the 18th hole, we both hit good drives. Lew's second shot went just over the green and stopped about a foot short of the heavy rough. He played a good chip back that hit the hole and finished a little more than two feet away. I hit my second shot 25 feet above the hole and left my first putt short about the same distance as Worsham's. I had been putting poorly all week with an old Blue Goose putter, the only time I've ever putted with a mallet-head in a tournament. It was a terrible putter. I couldn't get it to set square to the ball; it kept falling over closed. Well, I thought I was away, so I got up to hit the putt with my old faithless Blue

Goose when I hear Worsham say, "Hey, what are you doing?"

"I'm putting out," I said.

"Are you sure you're away? I think maybe I am and have first shot," said Worsham.

So we called over the referee, Ike Grainger, who was later president of the USGA. "I believe it's in the rules that once a man has started to putt, he's entitled to finish," I told him, but he didn't answer me. In retrospect I should have been more forceful because the rules allow you to continue putting in stroke play. While an 18-hole playoff between two players essentially becomes like match play, the rules for stroke play still apply. (In match play, whoever is away on the green has the honor.) Regardless, the delay is what hurt me, not the ruling. Grainger took out a tape measure and measured our putts. Mine was 30½ inches away and Worsham's was 30 inches. I can still see that damn putt in my mind today. Lew had an easy uphill putt, but mine was downhill with a left-to-right break. I didn't hit it hard enough, and it broke out about two inches. Worsham rammed his right in the middle. Was what Worsham did gamesmanship? Yeah, I think so, but I hold no grudge against him. I'm a pro and I should have been able to handle it.

As I later said, "Lew did what he needed to do if he was to win, and if a man can't defend himself against a smart psychologist, he belongs in the clubhouse playing gin, not out there with big-time cutthroats."

Some forms of gamesmanship are a little more inventive. I heard about one used in the final round of the Indianapolis Country Club championship in the late 1950s. Pete Dye, the architect, was 3 down with four holes to play against Robert Bowen, a good amateur golfer and member of Pine Valley. As they stood on the 15th tee, Dye stopped in the middle of his backswing and looked up in the sky for several seconds.

"I see a vision, " he said.

Bowen looked up, too. Finally he said, "What's going on here?"

"I see a vision," continued Dye, "that I'm going to win this hole with a par. Then win the next hole with a birdie. Then win 17 with a par. And on 18, you're not even going to finish the hole."

And that is exactly what happened.

Have you heard about the time that Babe Ruth used a little gamesmanship in a golf match against Dizzy Dean in 1933 at Clearwater, Fla.? Dizzy had just taken up the game, but he loved to gamble, and Babe was willing to accommodate him.

"I'm giving him five strokes a side, but I've got a secret weapon," Ruth confided to a friend.

When they got to the country club, Babe asked Dizzy's wife, Pat, to follow them around on the course. "The walk will do you good," he told her. Dizzy had no comment.

The first hole went quietly, but on the second Dizzy hit a couple of bad shots and Pat said, "Dear, you're ducking."

That was all Dean needed to hear. He blew up like an overheated still. "Ducking, hell!" he snarled. "Who invited you on this rabbit shoot anyhow?"

Ruth laughed all the way to the bank that day.

I was guilty of a bit of gamesmanship myself in a money match with Bobby Cole during a practice round before the Masters a few years ago. I was 1 down, but not for long, coming to the par-5 13th hole, a dogleg left with a creek and a forest of pine trees running down the whole left side.

"When I was your age, son," I told Bobby on the tee. "I used to just haul off and hit me a big ol' hook over them trees. Left me a middle iron to the green."

Bobby looked at the trees, grabbed his driver and hit a terrific shot that climbed and soared—and clattered around in the top of the trees, dropping into the creek.

"I jumped all over that one, Sam," said Bobby. "How did you ever knock it over those trees?"

"Son," I said, "when I was your age, those trees were only this high."

A common ruse I've seen used over the years is to throw off a player with club selection. Dutch Harrison was great at disguising a 6-iron as a 4-iron and putting an LPGA swing on the ball. I saw him do it once on a par 3 in a match against Dave Ragan. Dave couldn't help noticing what Dutch hit, so he went back to his bag, changed clubs and flew the green by 20 yards. It cost him the match.

I've always been a bit of a bag hawk myself; I like to see what the other fellow is hitting, but I don't let it throw me off. I learned that lesson playing with Willie MacFarlane in an early Metropolitan Open in Essex County, N.J. On one hole I watched Willie hit a 4-iron onto the green, but the shot couldn't have been any more than 145 yards. I took out an 8-iron and knocked mine on. Walking off the green, I said, "Willie, why did you hit so much club?"

"Laddie," he said, "I saw you watching, and I wanted to teach you a lesson. Don't ever pay attention to what the other man uses."

My favorite brand of gamesmanship is to keep pumping up the ego of the other guy. Every good shot he hits is a great one. Lay on the compliments with a ladle. Ask him about his good shots. What was he trying to do? When you win a hole, it's because of that lucky bounce or that lucky putt. This begins to wear on a fellow's nerves. I remember using this tactic in a match against Leonard Dodson many years ago. I outdrove him by 20 yards off the first tee. When we got to our balls, Dodson said, "Who's that up ahead?"

"Mine," I said.

"What the hell did you hit?" he said.

"It must have hit a rock," I said.

The same routine went on again at the second hole, and again I explained that it must have hit a rock. I outdrove him by 30 yards on the third hole and again made the same remark about hitting a hard spot. On the fourth hole, he beat me to the explanation.

"I know, I know," he said, "it must have hit a rock. All I can say is that this golf course has more rocks than a quarry and you're the only man that's ever found them."

Gamesmanship has been around as long as golf has been played, and in some ways I think it adds a little charm to the game. Charles Price, the writer, once told me about a book written almost a century ago by the British Amateur champion Horace Hutchinson, called *Hints on the Game of Golf*, which advised players about the subtle art of gamesmanship:

"If your adversary is badly bunkered, there is no rule against your standing over him and counting his strokes aloud, with increasing gusto as their number mounts up; but it will be a wise precaution to arm yourself with a niblick before doing so, so as to meet him on equal terms.

"If your adversary is a hole or two down, there is no serious cause for alarm in his complaining of a severely sprained wrist or an acute pain resembling lumbago, which checks his swing. Should he happen to win the next hole, these symptoms will in all probability be less troublesome.

"If you find yourself being outplayed by the excellent iron approaches of your adversary, it is sometimes a good plan to say to him, in a tone of friendly interest, 'Really you are playing your iron wonderfully well today—better than I ever saw you play it before. Can you account for it in any way?' This is likely to promote a slight nervousness when he next takes his iron in his hand; and this nervousness is likely, if the match is at all a close one, to be of considerable service to you. There is no rule to prevent your doing this; only after a time will people stop playing with you."

10

How to Deal With Cheaters

When Don January and I were partners in the Legends of Golf senior tournament back in 1982, we made every putt from Onion Creek Country Club to the Austin capitol building. Don had 13 birdies and I had 14. We put distance between us and the field like thoroughbreds pulling away from a herd of mules. I remember at one point in the final round I made long putts for birdies on the 15th and 16th holes, and January turned to me and said, "Man, how many do you want to win by, Sam?"

"You never know," I told him, "them folks up ahead might be cheatin'."

I was kidding, of course. Golf is the cleanest of all sports that I know about, at least on the professional level. The pros play right according to Hoyle, and 99 percent of amateurs are the same way. When I play a man—whether he's a pro or a 90-shooter—I expect him to follow the law to a letter.

When a guy makes an honest mistake, you should give him the benefit of the doubt. I remember in the first tournament I ever won I almost got disqualified for breaking the rules. It was the 1936 West Virginia Open at Guyan Country Club near Huntington. There had been so much rain that the course turned into a quagmire. The tees, which were dirt to start with, became mud puddles. In the first round I just learned to work my feet down deep into the mud, cut short my backswing and slow down my tempo. I shot 65 and was the only one to break 80. Of course, it wasn't that strong a field. In the second round, along about the 10th hole, a fellow came running down from the clubhouse and said, "I've been sent out to tell you guys to move off the dirt tees onto the grass beside the markers."

"Are you sure?" I said.

"Yeah, they sent me out," he said.

So I started teeing off from the grass, and later a writer named Fred Burns came over and said, "Hey, you better get back on the tees. They didn't change any rules."

When I finished, the tournament committee wanted to disqualify me for not playing from the markers. "If I'm disqualified, so are you, you, you and you," I told them, pointing at the pros around the room, "because you guys played from the grass, too." After a little conference, they decided to wash out the round completely. I still ended up winning the tournament, my first as a pro.

Any breaking of rules you see on tour is almost always by accident or ignorance. I remember years ago winning a tournament in Miami that I later learned may have been influenced by a gambler. Chandler Harper and a friend of his had a bet on me with a bookie, and they were following my group the last round. It was a cold day, and they noticed that this one fellow in a camel's-hair coat was hit by my ball on one hole. The ball bounced back on the green. A few holes later I sailed another iron shot over the green, and don't you know it hits this same guy and bounces back close to the hole. I didn't know what was going on. After I won, Chandler and his friend went to collect their bet, and who is first in line but the man in the camel's-hair coat.

Another time I was playing in the St. Paul Open when I got a telephone call in my hotel room at 12:30 in the morning.

"You Sam Snead?" the voice asked.

"Yeah, who are you?" I said, still groggy.

"Never mind, you keep playing. You are going to win this tournament."

"How in hell am I going to win? I'm 10 shots behind Lloyd Mangrum with 18 holes to go. Do you realize what time it is?"

"Don't worry about a thing. Just keep playing." And he hangs up.

I was in second place but 10 shots behind, so there was no way I could overtake Mangrum. Here, the same guy called Lloyd and threatened to shoot him if he won. Ol' Lloyd was one tough monkey, which this guy didn't figure. He won the tournament and we never heard from the thug who called. Mangrum was a pretty mean fellow himself, a man you wouldn't want to tangle with. He had a thin, black mustache that made him look like a riverboat gambler, which is what he thought he was. I knew him for 30 years and I didn't know him at all. I was in a restaurant once with him when he tripped over a man's foot. "Why the hell don't you keep your feet under the table?" he shouted. Then he took a sugar bowl and smashed the guy right in the face with it. The poor man didn't know what hit him.

That St. Paul Open was the only pro tournament I ever heard of that gamblers tried to fix. They know golf is too unpredictable. Unlike a horse race where there may be only three or four horses capable of winning the race, any one of 50 pros could win a golf tournament, and today there might be 100 possible winners.

Some cheating still goes on in the amateur ranks, though—that 1 percent I was telling you about. As the sportswriter Paul Gallico used to say, "If there is any larceny in a man, golf will bring it out." When the stakes get too high and golfers begin to play for more than they can afford, you have to watch for a little bit of this larceny. You know the other fellow is watching you.

If you see a rule being broken, you have to call it. The Rules of Golf say you're just as guilty if you witness it and look the other way. It's the golfing equivalent of leaving the scene of a crime. Too many golfers won't utter a peep until they get back to the locker room, and then they blast the guy behind his back. Maybe he didn't break the rule, or maybe he doesn't know the rule. Give him the chance to defend himself. You can ruin a man's reputation by not calling it on him.

If your opponent is a repeated offender, don't play with him. Or if he's the only game in town and you have to keep playing with him, watch him like a hawk. Remember the old saying: "Cheat me once, shame on you. Cheat me twice, shame on me."

The biggest cheating offense I see is golfers stepping behind their ball in the rough to improve the lie. I caught a fellow doing it the other day and said to him, "What are you doing?"

"Nothing," he said.

"You stepped behind your ball," I said.

"Oh, no, I didn't."

"That was the second time I saw you do it today. If you want to play, OK. If you want to call off the bet, that's OK, too. But if you do it again, you lose the match."

He called off the bet, and that's the last time he'll get his cheating claws into me.

I play with a guy all the time back home at the Lower Cascades Course who cheats his way around the course. And he's a judge, an officer of the law. We call him the Hangin' Judge. He's always stepping behind his ball or teeing it up in the rough. "You SOB, you wouldn't last nine holes on the PGA Tour," I tell him. "You're never happy unless you think you're taking advantage of someone."

If you don't keep your eye on him in a bunker, the Hangin' Judge takes a couple of practice backswings brushing away the sand from behind the ball. Now he's got a trough in the sand and he can just clip out his ball. "You play those trap shots pretty good," I tell him when I see him do it. Caught red-handed, he just grins and picks up his ball.

I remember playing one time with a couple of old boys you had to keep your eye on. The one guy couldn't find his ball, so we went ahead, hit our approaches and walked to the green. All of a sudden we hear, "Fore!" and a ball comes whizzing by my ear onto the green.

"I found it," the guy hollers.

"That cheatin' bastard," the other fellow says, "I got his ball in my pocket."

I've never caught anybody doing it, but I'm told some cheaters put Vaseline on the face of their clubs. It cuts down on the sidespin on your shots and you hit the ball straighter. The rules make it illegal to put any foreign substance on the clubface, but these cheaters are regular Gaylord Perrys when it comes to hitting spitballs.

"Some people say the grease is psychological," says one gambler who uses it. "Well, the people who say that must not have tried it. Grease puts 10 to 20 extra yards on a shot. If you happen to be playing somewhere grease is not familiar, they'll look at you funny if they catch you doing it. I told some people one time I was putting on the grease to keep my clubs from rusting. It hadn't rained there in two years."

Another type of cheater is the guy who phonies up his handicap. Like the joke Bob Hope tells about a 12-handicapper who complains about his 10-handicap friend: "How about that guy? He gives me a stroke a side and I still have to shoot 68 to beat him. The lousy sandbagger."

I've already mentioned that you should never bet against strangers, and consider everybody a stranger until you've played with him a dozen times. The USGA is cracking down on sandbaggers with its new computerized handicapping network and the Slope System, which adjusts your handicap according to the difficulty of the course you're playing. I'd like to think sandbaggers will be a thing of the past, but they'll be around as long as people cheat on their income tax. It's in their nature.

I remember one time a caddie cheated for me and I didn't even know it. Jerry Barber and I were playing a money match against Dow Finster-wald and Arnold Palmer in a practice round for a tournament in Las Vegas. I had a little Greek boy for a caddie. On about the sixth or seventh hole, we walk up to our shots in the fairway, and there he was with my ball in his hands cleaning it.

"What the hell are you doing?" Palmer said.

"Mr. Sam wanted his ball cleaned on every hole," the boy explained.

"Well, goddamn, wait until he gets on the green," said Arnie.

I had to laugh at that one. They let me drop it and there was no penalty.

The only time I ever out-and-out cheated on the course was in a match against Mason Rudolph for the television show "World Championship Golf" in 1960. And the funny thing is I was trying to throw the match, not win it. On the 12th hole I looked in my bag and noticed a 2-wood I thought I'd left in my locker. "Oh, no," I said to myself, "I've got 15 clubs"—one more than the rules allow you to carry.

The match was about even to that point, although actually as soon as I discovered the 15th club I'd lost 10 and 8. I didn't know what to do. The producer of the show, Fred Briskin, had been very nice to me and I didn't want to embarrass him or the sponsor, so on the 16th hole I decided I was going to tank the match. The only problem was that Rudolph started hacking it around so bad I couldn't give him a hole. We were even going into the 16th hole, which I had to four-putt to lose to Mason and go 1 down. He bogeyed the par-3 17th and I hit my tee shot so close I had to make a par to square the match. Then I three-putted 18 to lose 1 down. "If Mason had hit his drive in the rockbed on 18, I would have been in a real mess," I told reporters at the time. "I'd have had to shank a couple."

I got into a lot of trouble over that one. I had to apologize to the PGA and to the network. The sponsor of the show, a razor-blade company, withdrew its support from "World Championship Golf." Mason accused me of really having 14 clubs in my bag and only making up the excuse as an alibi. Finally it blew over, but the whole episode reminded me always to play within the rules.

Leave the cheatin' for the cheaters. And keep one eye on those boys all the time.

11

How to Collect a Bet

Ow do you collect a bet? This should be a short story. If a guy doesn't pay you when you beat him, don't play him anymore. Consider a loss the cost of your education. I've never been one for breaking a fellow's knuckles. Hell, if it comes to that, you're playing for too damn much money. But I did hear once of a bet between two pros in a practice round for the 1972 Gardena Valley Open that couldn't be paid. That night the welsher got beaten up in the parking lot and had to pull out of the tournament with a broken arm.

Another time I heard that Charlie Sifford got involved with Clayton Heafner in a bet he couldn't afford. In those days Charlie was a caddie in Charlotte, N.C., and Heafner was the club pro. When it became apparent that Sifford couldn't pay off, Heafner threw him into a lake. I wasn't there so I can't attest to the truthfulness of this tale, but I do believe Heafner was capable of it. I was with him one time when an internal revenue man put a search on his person, looking for how much cash he was carrying; I guess he owed them money. When the internal revenuer came back the next day, Heafner called his lawyer.

"That little SOB is back and he wants to search me again," said Heafner.

"He can only search you one time," said his lawyer.

"You're sure? Because I'm about to throw the bastard through the screen door."

"You don't have to throw him through the door, but he can't search you."

So Heafner got off the phone and said to the guy, "You better be out of here by the time I count to five. One...two...."

And he was gone. I wouldn't put it past ol' Clayton to put that internal revenuer through the screen door or Charlie Sifford into the lake.

Golf has had a history of unpaid debts. I remember reading about a bunch of rich people who got 100 to 1 from London bookmakers on Bobby Jones winning the Grand Slam in 1930 and never collected a farthing. And a few years earlier, Al Wallace, a Detroit gambler, bet $2,000 at 20 to 1 on Walter Hagen to win the 1922 British Open. His receipt read "$40,000 to $2,000," but when Hagen won Wallace only got his two G's back with no profit. When you bet with bookies, you're lucky to escape with the golf shirt on your back.

I've been swindled a few times on nassau bets, too, but there's not much you can do about it. "I'll pay you when I get it," they always say. Then after a while, it becomes a joke. "Oh, yeah, I'll give it to you one of these days." My only advice is to keep reminding the welsher and don't play him again until you get your money.

Bob Hope tells a funny story about his old rival Bing Crosby, who was known to make an opponent wait for the payoff. In an exhibition ahead of the San Antonio Open, Hope and Jimmy Demaret played a $10 nassau against Crosby and Byron Nelson. Bing and Byron had a bad day and lost six ways. "We got busy after the round," Hope says, "and nothing was said about the money. A couple of months later I'm browsing in the golf shop at Lakeside when suddenly Crosby walks in. He doesn't know I'm there. Bing exchanges a $100 bill for five 20s. I reach out from behind a post, grab three of them and say, 'Dad, that's for San Antonio.' We had a footrace around Lakeside."

12

Oh, Calcuttas!

Today there's a saying that the leading money winner on the PGA Tour is charity. Back when I was in my prime, 30 or 40 years ago, the leading money winner wasn't charity and it wasn't a touring pro, either. The guy who collected the most money was the gambler who owned the tournament winner in the calcutta pool.

A calcutta is a form of betting on golf in which the field is divided into teams and each team is auctioned off to the highest bidder. Depending on the local rules, the team sometimes is permitted to buy back a 50 percent share by paying its owner one-half the purchase price. Most of the fun is in the bidding itself. It usually takes place in the festive atmosphere of a crowded, smoke-filled room of jovial golfers plied with free liquor. The payoff is normally win, place and show, with the pool being divided among the owners of the first-, second- and third-place finishers.

One of the biggest calcuttas I ever heard of was in the 1929 U.S. Amateur at Pebble Beach, where the total pool exceeded $200,000. Most people say it also had the biggest upset. Bobby Jones, the reigning U.S. Open champion and the favorite, was auctioned off at $60,000, but Johnny Goodman eliminated him in the first round. There must have been some sorrowful souls around the 19th hole that day. The local sportswriters supposedly had a rough time, too. Jim Thorpe, the Olympic gold medal winner, not the tour pro, was hired as a bouncer to guard the booze in the pressroom. He knew all the Eastern writers there—like Grantland Rice, Bill Corum, Damon Runyon, Westbrook Pegler—and they had all the liquor they wanted, but every time a California writer bellied up to the bar, Thorpe shoved him aside.

Probably the all-time leading money winner for calcuttas was Frankie Laine, the singer, who made a fortune betting on Gene Littler in the Tournament of Champions, then played in Las Vegas. Laine bid $13,000 for Gene in 1955 and collected $72,900 when he won. Laine bid $16,500 for Gene the next year and he won again, collecting $68,120. Then Laine really hit the lottery. He bid $15,500 in 1957 and The Machine won the tournament for the third year in a row, with a $100,100 jackpot.

I played with Littler one of those years, and he really was unstoppable. I'll never forget on one hole he hit his putt about two feet past the hole and it turned around and rolled back down the hill into the hole. If I didn't know better, I'd have thought Frankie Laine loaded the dice.

The Masters, for years, ran its own calcutta, as did a lot of pro tour events. But in the mid-1950s the big money pools shifted to the smaller pro-ams and amateur events around the country. Because the players were not as well known, sandbagging became a problem as low handicappers entered the tournaments with phonied high handicaps. The most notorious incident occurred in 1955 at the Deepdale Golf Club on Long Island, N.Y. The calcutta pool was small-time, $45,000, but the cheaters deserved a long stretch in San Quentin. Two Massachusetts golfers with posted handicaps of 17 and 18 bought themselves in the calcutta. After they won the $16,000 first prize easily, it was learned they both had 3 handicaps. When the fraud became public, many leading amateurs and the U.S. Golf Association campaigned to ban calcuttas. They have disappeared completely from the pro tour and, with rare exceptions, from amateur events, too.

When the USGA learned that some clubs again were running calcuttas in the late 1960s, the governing body released a statement from

Richard Tufts who spoke for the USGA executive committee during the Deepdale scandal: "The executive committee feel at present that the association should not attempt disciplinary action against member clubs which disagree with USGA policy. There can be so many kinds and degrees of gambling that it would be impossible to draw a fair line between the harmful and the seemingly harmless. Further, the committee is reluctant to intrude in the private affairs of a club, which theoretically is an extension of the homes of its members.

"However, some clubs do not fully appreciate the evils inherent in gambling. Too frequently gambling tournaments coming to the committee's attention have spawned some unpleasantness, if not dishonesty—such things as falsification of handicaps and scores, evasion of Rules of Golf, payoffs to players (so-called amateurs), attraction of persons of questionable motives, chicanery in various forms. These things seem almost inevitable where the object is not golf but money. Even in the small, seemingly well-controlled calcutta, the prospect of financial return has undoubtedly influenced some competitor to 'negotiate' for a higher handicap."

Mr. Tufts' objections to calcutta pools make a lot of sense to me. I personally am not a fan of that form of betting; it's as unpredictable as a horse race with a field of 144 horses. But if you insist on playing calcuttas, I offer two bits of advice: (1) Stay away from handicapped competitions. Only bet if everyone is playing scratch, and then bet on the best player. It's too easy for the cheater to fix his handicap. (2) Never take less than 8-to-1 odds. Calculate your bid versus the ultimate payoff. If the total pool is $1,000, with 50 percent going to the winner, you should bid no more than $60; at that price, winning would yield slightly better than an 8-to-1 payoff ($60 \times 8 = 480$). I prefer head-to-head betting myself. That way I can keep my eye on the opposition.

13

13

How Long is a Gimme?

I'd like to own the real estate that was given to President Eisenhower on the greens. I played quite a bit with Ike when he was in office, and I don't remember him ever holing a three- or four-footer. "I think I can make this," he'd say. "That's good, Mr. Prez," somebody always piped up. He probably would have missed half of them, but we all knew that gimmes were just one of the perks of his job.

President John Kennedy once played a match against Chris Dunphy, the longtime chairman of Seminole Golf Club in Florida. On the first hole, Kennedy hit a good second shot that finished three feet from the hole. When they arrived on the green, the President looked to Dunphy for a concession, but Dunphy said nothing.

"You're certainly going to give me this, aren't you?" Kennedy said.

"Make a pass at it," said Dunphy. "I want to see your stroke."

"OK," said Kennedy, "but let's keep moving. I've got a meeting right after our round with the internal revenue director."

"The putt's good," said Dunphy wisely. "Pick it up."

When Richard Nixon was Vice President, he came down to play at the Greenbrier one time with me and the late Arthur Hill, who was chairman of the board of Greyhound. The Vice President and I didn't have a bet, but he was playing Mr. Hill a $2 nassau. Arthur Hill was the kind of guy who wouldn't give you the time of day, so I knew there wouldn't be too many concessions on the greens. On the opening hole, Nixon rolled his first putt a couple of feet past the hole and looked up expectantly at Hill, who didn't breathe a word. Finally, Nixon said, "I'm not used to putting these, Art. Usually they give me two- or three-footers."

"For my money, Mr. Vice President," said Hill, "you putt everything out."

The funny thing was Nixon missed almost every short putt he had. He lost the front nine, the back nine, the match and all the presses. Needless to say, he didn't hand out any ambassadorships that day.

But Arthur Hill was right. The best rule on the greens is to putt out everything. Don't give anything and don't expect to be given anything. I've seen the best players in the world miss putts inside two feet, so no putt is a sure thing. If there's any kind of a sidehill or downhill contour, you'd be surprised how many "gimmes" can be missed. Certainly when you're playing for a lot of dough, you should hole everything. From four feet to two feet to one inch— putt it into the hole. It only takes a moment and it avoids all arguments.

Of course, this policy isn't always feasible. If you're playing for a couple of bucks among friends or if you're entertaining a client or your boss, the milk of human kindness might flow more generously. But you should decide the policy for concessions on the first tee.

Walter Hagen, I'm told, used to try to psych-out his opponents by conceding longish putts on the early holes and then, later in the match, not give a short putt. The victim of this strategy would wait for Walter to say, "Pick it up." When no concession came, he'd begin to worry that the putt might be harder than it looked. According to legend, the poor fellow would borrow too much break, his two-footer never would touch the hole and the Haig would walk away with another PGA Championship. The story sounds good in the retelling, but I don't believe it. Hagen was too smart a player to give away such an edge in a close match. A missed putt early in the round is just as costly as one on the last hole. Each shot counts the same when the game is over.

In team matches, it's universally agreed that when one partner gives a putt, he is acting on behalf of the team and the other partner cannot retract the concession. As they say in some circles, a house divided don't win no pots. To eliminate any dissension in the ranks, I like to consult with my partner before giving any putt that's longer than a few inches. A simple "What do you think, pard?" will save any hard feelings between players on the same side. By the way, the Rules of Golf specify that once a putt is conceded, even if the player putts it anyway and misses, the hole is completed and the putt was good. However, don't put yourself in this embarrassing position. If your opponent utters the two most welcome words in golf—"That's good"—pick it up and go to the next tee.

Never take anything for granted, though. A putt is not good—no matter its length—until either it's conceded or it's holed. This reminds me of a 36-hole match my friend Bill Campbell played in the final of the 1952 Canadian Amateur at the Capilano Golf and Country Club in Vancouver. Bill and his opponent, who shall remain nameless, had been conceding short putts to one another all day—at least until they came to the 34th hole. Campbell stood 2 up with three to play. Both players had putts of about three feet—only Campbell was putting for a par 3 and his opponent for a bogey 4. After the putts were measured and Campbell was judged to be inside, his opponent holed for a 4 and walked off the green to the next tee, taking the referee of the match with him. That left Campbell putting for the outright victory. Campbell missed. The ball stopped on the lip. Unthinking, he raked it back and tried the putt over again, making it the second time. Then he walked to the next tee.

"Did you make it?" his opponent said.

"What do you mean?" said Campbell.

"The little one, I didn't give it to you."

Bill realized that he had not holed out and informed the referee that he had lost the hole. Instead of being 2 up with two to play, he was only 1 up. His opponent birdied the next hole to square the match. On the 36th hole, Campbell had two putts to win, but three-putted to send the match into extra holes. He lost on the 37th hole. His lapse cost him the tournament, but Bill learned a lesson about golf and human nature that day. While his opponent wasn't much of a sportsman, there's no denying Campbell was wrong. As far as I know, and I've played a lot of golf with Bill, he's never made that same mistake again.

I remember a similar incident that happened back in the 1930s at a pro-am. This particular tournament took place at Seminole, in Palm Beach, Fla., where 20 or 30 of the top pros were paired with club members. A wealthy businessman named Earl T. Smith drew Lawson

Little as his partner. "If we win," he told Lawson, "I'll give you $5,000 and a Cadillac. If we finish second, I'll give you $3,000 and a Buick. If we finish third, I'll give you $2,000 and a Ford." Lawson was not accustomed to such philanthropy, so he was going to give Mr. Smith his best effort. The agreement was that Little would be the boss on the course and would make all the decisions. "Just remember," he told Smith, "everything has to be putted out. Don't back-hand or one-hand any putt. Don't take anything for granted."

The team of Little-Smith came to the 445-yard last hole needing a par 4 for first place. Both partners drove almost side by side. Little used a 1-iron and pushed his second into the deep bunker alongside the green, from which he skulled his ball into the ocean. Mr. Smith hit a good 4-wood to the front edge of the green and chipped up close. Lawson picked up and went to help his partner read the two-footer.

"One putt for a Cadillac, two putts for a Buick and three putts for a Ford," thought Little.

"Let's see, there's $118,000 in the calcutta pool with 70 percent for first place, 20 percent for second and 10 percent for third," thought Smith.

Smith addressed the ball and stood there frozen, unable to take the club back. Perspiration formed on his head. His knees began to flutter. His face turned blue.

Seeing his partner's predicament, Little called time out and tried to comfort him. "Look," he said, "back off and relax. Take a couple of practice strokes, set up, waggle once and hit the putt. Even if you miss, we're still in the money."

With a hundred of his friends in the gallery, Smith returned to his ball and again his hands turned to concrete. A minute went by. Little again called for a conference. He decided to take a new tack. "Don't worry about it," he said. "Just walk back, and as you're walking, hit the ball."

Once again, Smith approached the putt, this time with Little's new strategy in mind. Unaccustomed to putting on the run, he nearly whiffed the ball, catching it just on the top. The ball made a weak little hop, rolled up and stopped on the edge of the hole.

Just then Lawson yelled, "No, Earl, don't do it!" But it was too late. Smith had reached over with his putter and dragged the ball back to try it one more time. Realizing he hadn't holed out, Smith hit the ball again while it was still rolling. After all the penalty strokes were assessed, the team of Little-Smith limped off the green. Smith didn't collect on the calcutta and Little didn't even get a Ford.

14

Quitters Never Win...

That old saw my daddy taught me—"Winners never quit and quitters never win"—was proved at least half wrong in the 1940 New Orleans Open. I was ahead of Jimmy Demaret by a couple of shots in the last round going into the par-3 15th hole. Jimmy topped his tee shot and then hit the next one fat. For all his happy-go-lucky antics, Demaret had a quick temper, and it didn't take much to set him off. Ready to pack it in, he made a one-handed swipe at the ball; it trickled onto the green and he two-putted for a double bogey.

"You can have the bleeping money," he said to me as we walked off the green.

I should have kept my mouth shut, but I didn't. I reminded him of what my daddy taught me and I explained the mathematics of a birdie-birdie-birdie finish.

Sure enough, he birdied the next three holes and I ran into a disaster.

As I addressed my ball off the back edge of the 17th green, it rolled over costing me a penalty stroke, which shook me up pretty good. I hit a lousy chip and missed the putt, taking a double bogey. "Demaret Beats Snead by One," the headlines read.

That tournament may have been the exception to the rule about quitters. But actually, Jimmy only quit momentarily. By the time he walked from the 15th green to the 16th tee, he was 100 percent again, trying to beat my ass. You're allowed to quit from green to tee, but never from tee to green.

I used to be a quitter back when I first joined the tour in the 1930s. And like most quitters, I had a good reason to quit. The tournament committee kept pairing me with Jimmy Thompson, the long-ball hitter, to put on a show for the galleries. Thompson was the world's longest driver in those days; I was pretty long, but he could outdrive me by 20 yards when he caught one. Every day we were paired together was a long-driving championship. It wasn't long before I couldn't break 70, and I wasn't making enough to cover room and board. Finally, when they paired us together again in the 1937 Pasadena Open, I threatened to walk off and the PGA threatened to suspend me, so I played. I shot 41 going out and was on my way to an 80 when I picked up and withdrew. The newspapers had a field day. I left town and went to Pinehurst, N.C., and once again I picked up in the middle of a bad round. I figured the galleries didn't pay to see me play poorly, and I wasn't about to make a fool of myself in front of a thousand people, so why not quit? I was wrong, of course. I was acting like a loser. Winners find reasons not to quit.

Billy Casper is an example of a golfer who made himself a winner because he never quit. If you watched Casper and, say, Gene Littler hit balls on the practice range, you would have to conclude that Gene was half again the better player. But somehow Casper won 22 more tournaments than Littler. Billy always had the moxie to keep plugging away even when things were going wrong. Gene always seemed to have the attitude, "Oh, well, this is a job. I don't feel like playing anyway, but I have to do it to make money to buy those antique cars of mine." Like Hogan, Littler never appeared to enjoy playing golf. When he got a few bad bounces, he was more willing to say, "The hell with it. This is not day." I don't mean to imply that Gene is a quitter. Anybody who beats cancer is no quitter, but let's just say he didn't always handle adversity well on the golf course. When things went wrong, he'd rather be home polishing his cars.

I'd recommend imitating Billy Casper's attitude on the course. The key to his success is that he never allowed himself to hit two bad shots in a row. Whenever he foozled a chip or missed a drive, he concentrated real hard on the next one. Quitters often let one bad shot lead to another and another, and before they know it the match is over. Casper could afford to be patient with himself, because he was such a good short-game player that he could reclaim any lost shot with a good chip or putt, and he knew it.

The big mistake I see a lot of golfers making is that they hit a what-the-hell shot after their opponents knock one close. It usually happens on a par 3 when the opponent hits his ball up against the hole. From the tee it looks like he's got a gimme. Actually he's about 10 feet away. Now the foolhardy player figures, what the hell, he has to try to hole his tee shot—and he ends up burying it in the bunker. Be realistic. The odds are that your opponent is going to make a 3, not a 2. Make sure you get your ball on the green, all the better if it's close.

I remember falling into this trap once in the International Four-Ball at Miami; Ralph Guldahl and I were partners in a match against Billy Burke and Craig Wood. On the eighth hole, a par 3 over water, Wood's shot covered the flag and stopped about three feet from the hole. I went for broke and knocked my ball in the pond, but it was partially submerged and I thought I still could play it.

"Give it a kiss," said my partner. "Pick it up."

I wasn't about to quit even though the odds were a thousand to one against my saving the hole. I took off my right shoe, sunk my foot into the mud, settled over the ball and took a mighty swing. The ball popped up in the air and came straight down like an Otis Elevator into the hole. Wood gave me a sideways glance without saying a word, stepped up to his three-footer and missed it. My daddy was right after all about quitters and winners.

15

How to Concentrate for 18 Holes

I've got about 30 chickens on my farm near The Homestead in Virginia, and when it's feeding time I'm always amazed at the concentration level of those birds. When they light on a handful of chicken feed, nothing else in the world is important to them. All animals are good concentrators. They think, as my sixth grade English teacher used to say, in the present tense. They only worry about the moment at hand and disregard everything that has come before or will come after. We golfers could learn a lesson from those chickens.

The key to good concentration is to concern yourself only with the here and now. You don't have to concentrate for four hours when you play 18 holes. Just start the clock a few seconds before each shot. Concentrating shouldn't be difficult. It's like pleasant daydreaming about a wonderful place you've been. Don't let negative thoughts creep in. Consider the lie of the ball. Check the distance. Decide what kind of shot you're going to hit. Select your club. Think target, and swing away. The whole process should take less than 30 seconds. All you're doing is telegraphing your muscles what to do.

As Yogi Berra used to say, "The game is 90 percent mental and the other half is physical." That's why Jack Nicklaus has always done well. He's the best at concentration that I have ever seen. I once asked him, "Why didn't you stop when that camera clicked as you were over the ball?"

"I didn't hear it," he said.

Some golfers have mule ears; they are distracted by butterflies in parallel fairways. I used to be able to block out everything, but as I've grown older I get distracted easier. It seems to me that recently Nicklaus has had to back away from shots more often, too. Maybe it is age.

Ben Hogan was good at keeping himself on an even keel for 18 holes. I always attributed that to his early training as a professional card dealer back in Texas. If you do that for a living, you learn pretty quickly to control your emotions and not show your feelings. I could never tell what Hogan was thinking. He just kept puffing away on his cigarettes. The only thing you could tell was that some shots were harder than others—some were one-cigarette shots and others were two-cigarette shots. I bet if you had hooked him up to a cardiac unit while he played, his heart would have been beating at one pace, whether it was the drive off the first tee or the putt to win everything on 18. Byron Nelson was the same way. Jimmy Demaret used to say that Nelson was so cold-blooded. "If Byron ever gave you a transfusion, you'd catch pneumonia."

Walter Hagen may have had the best temperament I've ever seen. He always gave the impression that he was in control of the situation. He had a great ability to turn a 77 into a 67. Hagen was smart enough to realize that he was going to get some good breaks and some bad ones; he was going to hit some good shots and some bad ones, and he never let either good or bad outcomes surprise him. He played like those chickens in my hen house, always in the present tense.

A fellow who is not as well known as these others but who had a terrific ability to concentrate was Bud Ward. When he stood over the ball it looked as if sparks came off his eyes. He could stare a putt into the hole. He must have been saying to himself, "It's going in. It's going in." I've shot a lot of polecats during hunting season, and they have eyes that shine in the dark, but I've never seen another set of sparklers like Bud Ward's.

I got some good advice from an old Scottish caddie once who told me to make my game as "storm-proof" as I can, so my concentration would stick even under the worst circumstances. Like those debutantes who learn to walk with books on their heads, I've always tried to maintain an even temperament throughout my round. Harold Bell, my old football coach back at Valley High School in Virginia, gave me another good piece of advice. He said, "I've known men who could get mad enough to fight a rattlesnake and give it two bites headstart, but they lost more fights than they won. A man who stays cool-mad will beat you every time."

That's a wonderful expression, cool-mad. I've remembered it since the first time I heard Harold Bell use it. It's OK to get hot. Even the game's greatest sportsman, Bobby Jones, once wrote, "To the finish of my golfing days I encountered emotions which could not be endured with the club still in my hands." Even Bobby Jones heaved a club in his day, and I've sure been guilty of drop-kicking a few in mine. But never, never hit a shot in anger. Get all the meanness out of you before addressing the ball.

I used to be a great one for fits of rage until I almost broke my foot in the British Open the year I won at St. Andrews. My approach shot to one of those big double-greens ended up on the wrong green, 60 yards from the hole. My first putt came up 40 feet short. I got so mad I whacked my putter against my foot, bashing in the cap of my alligator golf shoe and almost breaking my big toe. It hurt so bad I had to take my shoe off on the next hole, which gave the gallery a good laugh. It wasn't the last time I kicked my putter, but I learned to be a little more gentle about it.

Nothing breaks your concentration like a temper tantrum. And nothing gives an opponent a quicker charge than to see you lose your cool. Golf requires too much thinking and coordination to be played when you're mad. It's similar to boxing; a fighter likes to get the other guy hopping mad because he burns out faster.

If there's one quality that will help your concentration and temperament on the course, it is patience. When you hit a dumb shot or when an opponent does something to fry your innards, just take a deep breath and count to 10. And if that doesn't work, go ahead and throw a club. Just make sure nobody is in your way and you toss it in the direction you're walking. When you get to your next shot, get your mind in the present tense and stay cool-mad.

16

Match Play Tactics

The Lord hates cowards, but he's not fond of fools either. The trick is to play golf somewhere in between the coward and the fool—not too bold, but not too damn conservative.

I played my smartest golf in 1949 and 1950. I didn't try to outdrive anybody, just concentrated on keeping the ball in play. If I came to a par-5 hole with a 50-50 chance of getting on in two, and there was out-of-bounds right and water left, I laid up. More than half the time I pitched close and made a birdie anyway, but I stayed away from taking 6s and 7s. In 1950, I played 96 rounds with a 69.23 stroke average. And if I had left off five tournaments, like the U.S. Open, it might have been a 67 average.

I try to approach match play the same as stroke play—except that in match play I'm always keeping one eye on my opponent. Anybody who tells you that he just plays the course and ignores what his opponent is doing has got some bad moonshine. You mean to say that if the guy you're playing hits his tee shot OB, you're not going to play safe on your next shot? You're crazy if you don't.

Take for instance the time Cary Middlecoff and I are playing Harry Weetman and David Thomas in the Ryder Cup at Eldorado in Palm Springs. We were 1 down coming to the reachable par-5 last hole in an alternate-shot match. I drove my ball in the rough so Doc is trying to decide what club to hit to the green, which is flanked on both sides by water. Weetman gets up and hits his second into the hazard, looking to make a sure 6 or worse. Middlecoff is still thinking about what to hit.

"Doc," I says in a stage whisper, "if you don't lay up this thing short, I'm going to whack you in the leg. All we need is a 5 to win the hole."

So Doc chips out and I knock it on and we two-putt to win the hole and halve the match.

Of course, you shouldn't spend all your time worrying about what your opponent is doing. You don't need both eyes on him; one will do. When I play money matches against my friends at Pine Tree in Florida, where they're mostly 5-handicap and up, I try to walk the line between the coward and the fool and let them make the mistakes. I just play along and let it happen. When you have a bunch of matches against a lot of different opponents, you have to play as if it's a stroke-play tournament. As they say in cards, "You have to play the hand that's dealt you." But when there's an opening—say, you're also playing skins and you reach a par 5 in two with a reasonable putt for an eagle—go for the whip!

The best example I've ever seen of a player going for the whip was in the 1938 PGA Championship at Shawnee-on-the-Delaware, Pa. I played Paul Runyan, one of the shortest hitters of the day, in the 36-hole final. I figured it would be a cakewalk. I outhit Paul by 40 or 50 yards, which meant I could reach three of the four par 5s and he couldn't. Over 36 holes that gave me a six-stroke advantage. But somehow Paul saw an opening, went for that whip I was telling you about and played the par 5s in 6 under. On one hole I laid him a stymie, which means my ball finished between his ball and the hole on the putting green. He simply lofted his wedge over my ball and into the hole on the fly. I kept trying to make a comeback, but he kept burying me deeper until I ran out of holes. He beat me 8 down with seven to play, which is the most lopsided final in the history of the PGA. As Runyan's victim—and he has never let me forget it—I can attest to the value of tenacity and a good short game. Paul Runyan has both, as he continues to demonstrate even today on the senior tour.

Here are my 10 commandments for match play:

1. Play more conservatively early in a match. You should always play the percentages, but be especially careful on the opening holes until you get warmed up. Avoid unnecessary risks. A stupid mistake early can turn the momentum of the match against you.

2. When in doubt, check your opponent's lie. If you're trying to decide how to play your shot, take a moment to inspect your opponent's situation. This is especially important on a do-or-die decision. If he has a bad lie, take the safer route and aim for the middle of the green.

3. After winning a hole, concentrate on hitting a solid drive. Don't let up when you get ahead. The tendency for most golfers is to follow a winning putt with a poor drive. Collect your thoughts on the next tee, forget about sympathizing with your opponent and make solid contact.

4. When the momentum is going against you, change the pace of the match. If you're getting a stretch of bad bounces and you're behind, change the tempo of play. If the pace has been fast, walk slower, tie your shoes, tell a story, get a drink, change clubs—anything to slow down the match and throw off your opponent's rhythm. Likewise, if the pace has been slow, stop talking, walk faster, remark about the players waiting behind to play—again to throw off his natural rhythm. But remember, if anybody tries this tactic on you, ignore him and stick to the pace you're most comfortable with.

5. Always figure your opponent will make it. PGA Tour Commissioner Deane Beman says that when he watches his opponent standing over a long putt, he always thinks it will go in. Then on those rare instances when his opponent actually makes it, Beman isn't flustered. Most golfers are so surprised when their opponent makes an unlikely shot that they take several holes to recover.

6. Never give up on yourself. A good coach doesn't berate a player after a bad shot; the coach tells him that he's better than his performance indicates. "Now get out there and prove how good you really are," he says. In golf you have to be both player and coach. Don't get down on yourself after a bad shot; keep positive thoughts.

7. Don't get mad, get even. If you hit a bad shot, make sure the next shot is a good one. If you make a dumb decision, make sure the next decision is a smart one. Don't compound your mistakes.

8. When you decide to gamble, Katy bar the door. There's a saying in the backwoods: Never pull a gun unless you plan to use it, and never shoot except to kill. The trouble with many amateurs I see is that they're indecisive over the ball. If you're behind in a match, sometimes you have to play a low-percentage shot that might turn the tide. Once you've made the decision to gamble, take your club and hit hell out of it. Don't allow second guesses to creep into the top of your backswing. A faint heart never filled an inside straight.

9. Know the rules differences for match play. Over the last several years, the U.S. Golf Association has eliminated many of the differences between stroke and match play. Most golfers are ignorant of the rules, so the more you know, the better your advantage. For example, it used to be that you control your opponent's ball in match play when you're away on the green; you could ask him to mark and leave his ball to use it as a backstop. Today the rules have been changed so that he always has the option to mark and lift his ball regardless of your request.

10. Always keep the pressure on your opponent. Make the fellow you're playing earn every hole he wins. Never hand him a concession from the fairway. Even when he hits a spectacular shot, bear down and get your ball on the green and make him putt out. You'll be surprised how many holes you can win by getting up and down from around the green. But even if you don't win, you want him to feel the pressure of having to hit every shot. Over the course of 18 holes, it will take its toll.

A mistake I see golfers making all the time in match play is that they ease up when they get the lead. It reminds me of the time Willie Shoemaker stood up in his saddle and looked around down the stretch in the Kentucky Derby, and Bill Hartack on Iron Liege passed him at the finish line. One of the young fellows on the tour, Danny Edwards, has a good way of putting it. He's a race car driver in his spare time, and he compares playing under pressure to driving a car around a slick turn. The tendency for the average driver when he gets nervous is to touch the brakes—the way a golfer tries to play safely when he gets ahead—but hitting the brakes throws the weight to the front of the car and it will spin out. The experienced driver keeps his foot on the accelerator going around a turn, which keeps the weight in back and the car under control. The lesson here is stay aggressive when you get ahead in a match. I always figured the only thing better than being 5 up in a match was being 6 up and then 7 up. Bury your opponent if you get the chance. If you don't, quick enough you'll find yourself standing in a six-foot hole.

I remember playing with Mike Souchak at Greensboro one year when he had a big lead and started to play safe. He was five strokes ahead with four holes to go when he three-putted 15 to lose one shot. No. 16 is a long par 3, a tough SOB with a ditch around the green. He stepped up with a 2-iron in his hand, but all of a sudden the wind quit blowing, so he goes back and gets the 3-iron. Just as he gets to the top of his backswing, the breeze hits him in the face and he tries to give the 3-iron a little more juice. The ball balloons up in the air and comes down in the ditch and he eventually takes a 6. Then he three-putts 17 and misses a six-footer on the last hole to tie Billy Casper, leaving it a foot short downhill. Souchak lost the 1960 U.S. Open at Cherry Hills the same way, trying to play safe.

Average players sometimes lose their aggressiveness in partner matches, especially after their partners hit good shots. How many times have you watched your opponent hit it close on a par 3 and then scraped your ball into a bunker? Play your own game in four-ball matches; don't be overly concerned with how your partner is playing. Sure, if he's in trouble, you might want to play safer than normal. But don't let his ball dictate your strategy. If he hits one down the middle, don't automatically go for the big bomb off the tee. Remember, you always want to walk that thin line between the coward and the fool.

17

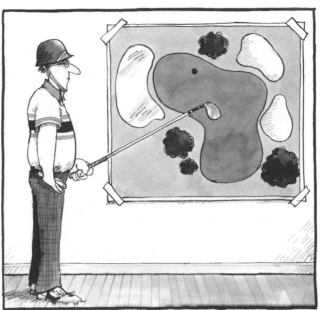

Strategy on the Greens

My strategy in playing matches is to get my ball in the hole first. I figure if I can post a score before my opponent, it will put more pressure on him. I learned this lesson the hard way in the 1953 U.S. Open at Oakmont when Ben Hogan and I were neck and neck going into the final day, but back then the U.S. Golf Association used to do some crazy things. Instead of pairing us together, they sent him off a couple of hours ahead of me. I've never known them to do this before or since. He had played nine holes before I even teed off. That was a hell of an advantage. Besides playing the greens before they got spiked up, he could post a score that I had to shoot at. He beat me good that day, but I've remembered the lesson. Whenever I have the chance, I always post my score first or hole my putt before the other guy.

One of the reasons I like to putt out is that I won't have time to think of ways to miss it. Everybody gets a little nervous on those short ones, so I feel the quicker I hit it the better chance I have of making it. Of course, you shouldn't rush. Take your time, but go ahead and knock it in.

In the Canadian Open years ago I remember Art Wall made this mistake playing against Billy Casper. Art had a long putt for a birdie that slid by the hole four feet. Billy had a 10-footer for a par. Instead of putting out, making his par and throwing the pressure on Casper, Art marked his ball. A few minutes before Billy must have figured he probably was going to lose the hole, but now he's thinking, "If I can get this baby in, he's apt to miss his." The advantage switched around. Naturally Billy made it and Art missed.

In stroke play the rules allow you to continue putting, but in two-ball match play the player who's away can make his opponent mark. Most of the time, though, a player would welcome his opponent to putt out, but I think that's a mistake. If the fellow I'm playing has a shorter putt than I have and we're both putting for the same score, I'll make him mark it and worry that dude while I putt mine.

In four-ball match play, the strategy is a little different with a partner. A common amateur mistake I see is when one player has a long putt for a birdie and his partner has a four- or five-footer for a par; the par-shooter usually goes first and misses, which puts double heat on his partner who three-putts to lose the hole. If the partner with the birdie putt is in three-putt range and/or if there's a reasonable chance that the par-putter could miss, mark the short putt and take a run at the birdie first. This drops the pressure level. If you miss the birdie, you still have two shots at a par. Saving strokes is your goal, not giving them away.

Gardner Dickinson and I were playing Gene Littler and Phil Rodgers, the San Diego Flashes, for a few bucks back in the 1960s. On one hole Rodgers and Littler made bogey 5s, and Gardner has an eight-footer for a birdie. He says to me, "I'm gonna drill this sucker right in the back of the hole."

"No, you're not," I said. "All we need is two putts for a 4. Just Ginsberg that thing up there close for a tap in."

In the meantime I had missed my birdie putt and left myself a 3½-footer. The green was real slick and Gardner knocks his four feet by. In these situations the strategy is to have the partner with the easier putt go first. Mine was uphill and shorter, so I putted and made it.

Two lessons should be learned here: (1) Don't go for a putt you don't need. Take two putts and walk away quietly. (2) Always have the fellow with the easier putt go first.

Gardner and I were playing another match against Dave Marr and

Tommy Jacobs that went into sudden-death. On the first extra hole, Dickinson has his ball about 25 feet away and I've got a 10-footer; Jacobs is 20 feet and Marr is out of the hole. Gardner is ready to putt, but I stop him.

"Let me go at this 10-footer," I says. "If I can make it, it'll really put the heat on Tommy."

It was an easy uphill putt, and the odds were a thousand to one I wouldn't three-putt. "I've been down this road a lot of times, trust me," I says to my partner.

I make mine, and Tommy gets up and leaves his downhill putt two feet short. It just goes to show, you should always try to make yours when you get the chance.

18

Tee-to-Green Strategy

When I was a little boy, my older brother Pete used to play a trick on me after dinner. "I'll race you up to bed," he'd yell and then dash to the stairs. I'd go tearing off after him, just managing to pass him at the doorway to our bedroom, which was pitch black because we had no upstairs electricity. Without my knowing it, Pete had rearranged the furniture. When I tried to dive into bed, I'd end up landing on the floor in the corner. I guess I was a slow learner because many a night I almost killed myself.

It's a lesson that helped me later in golf: Always check to see where the furniture is before you go diving head first. By "furniture," I mean, the lay of the land—both the targets and the hazards. I always believed in looking at where you want to hit the ball as well as where you don't want to hit it. Some might think this is a negative philosophy, but it's not. I don't dwell on the places to avoid, but I want to know where they are.

If there's out-of-bounds on the left, the last thing in the world you should be thinking over the ball is, "Don't hit it left." That should be your first thought before you even draw a club out of the bag. Then once you've identified the RED zone, as I call it, where under no circumstances you want to hit your shot, you look for the bail-out area, or the YELLOW zone. The yellow zone is where you can make your mistake; if you had to miss the ball there, at least you could play a recovery shot. Finally, you look for the GREEN zone, which is your target, where you want to hit the ball. Then you select your club and keep your mind in the green zone as you play the shot. This red-yellow-green approach can be applied to every shot you hit, from drives to putts. When you face a slick, 40-foot downhill putt, the red zone is short of the hole (because that would leave you another tricky downhiller that could cause you to four-putt), the yellow zone is past the hole (because your next putt would be a relatively easy uphiller) and the green zone is in the hole or within gimme range.

You have to decide for yourself what your personal red zones are, and they may change from round to round. If you're having trouble with sand play, for instance, bunkers may rate higher on your list of hazards to avoid.

Here's the order in which I generally look at red zones:

1. Out-of-bounds, the toughest of all penalties; it costs you two strokes.

2. Water hazards. Because you have to drop behind the hazard, you've cost yourself distance plus a penalty stroke; the net loss is about 1½ strokes.

3. Lateral water hazards. Because you have the added options of dropping on either side of the hazard two club-lengths from the point where the ball last crossed the margin of the hazard, you pick up some distance. It usually costs you one stroke.

4. Bushes or low-lying trees from which you have to take an unplayable lie; the net loss is one stroke.

5. Greenside or fairway bunkers. Depending on your skill in the sand, these may cost you one-half to one full stroke (or more, if you skull one into the tennis courts).

6. Heavy rough. The longer the hole the more important it is to keep your ball on the short grass. Figure heavy rough as a one-half to three-quarter stroke penalty.

7. Trees. As long as you can see through the limbs, you have some control over your shot trajectory and if you're not stupid, you should be able to cope with trees. The net loss should be no more than one-half stroke.

Let's go through the strategy of playing a few holes to see how this red-yellow-green approach works. For examples I've chosen the well-known Amen Corner of Augusta National: the par-4 11th, par-3 12th and par-5 13th holes.

No. 11, par 4, 455 yards.

How I play it: This is a long hole even for the pros, so I want to keep my tee shot down the left to take advantage of the downslope. The left side of the fairway is the green zone for me. The farther right I hit my drive, the longer my second shot is, but at least I have a shot over there. The right side of the fairway is the yellow zone. No man's land, the red zone, is the trees on the far left. They'd need a hound dog in there to find me.

How aggressive I am with my second shot is determined by the flag-stick position. A small water hazard guards the left front portion of the green, so I only go for the flag when it's in the middle to right half of the green. I remember one time when the hole was cut on the left side, Jackie Burke told Jimmy Demaret, "I hit me a 2-wood shot and put it right between the flag and the water, and nobody in the gallery clapped once!"

"No wonder," said Jimmy, "They wanted to know what idiot would hit it over there in the first place."

It's a big green, though. I've heard those stories about Ben Hogan saying, "If you see me on the green in two, you'll know I missed my second."

Meaning that he supposedly would hit his approach shot to the right of the green and play for a chip-and-putt par to avoid any chance of hitting in the water. That's crazy. The way Ben hit a 2-iron, he could have carved up that green like a pizza pie. I never knew him not to go for a green, on the 11th or anywhere else.

How you should play it: Eleven is a scary hole if you hit a big slice or hook, because the tee shot comes out of a narrow chute of trees. Even though it's a long hole, you should consider keeping your driver in the bag and hitting a 3- or 4-wood off the tee. The less loft a clubface has, the more pronounced your curve is going to be. Don't be fooled into going for the big bomb and ricocheting your drive off the trees—that's a sure way to hand the hole to your opponent on the tee. Your green zone is a long drive down the middle; your yellow zone is a short drive down the middle; either left or right out of the chute is red here.

Reconcile yourself to the fact that this hole is probably a par 5 for you. If you're playing with better golfers, you likely will get a handicap stroke. And with some good thinking you'll make a heck of a lot more 5-net-4s than your opponents will make gross 4s.

On the second shot, aim down the right side of the fairway (toward the 12th tee)—the green zone. The right rough is playable—the yellow zone. But the left side of the fairway or rough is definitely red because it forces you to carry your next shot over the water hazard. Then play a running pitch to the hole—short is better than long—and don't get the ball up in the air too high. Make your 5 and take your chances.

No. 12, par 3, 155 yards.

How I play it: Obviously where you don't want to hit it here is in Rae's Creek, the red zone. Anything short of the green tends to roll back into the hazard (unless it's trapped by the front bunker). The green zone is the green, and the yellow zone is just over the back of the green, either in the grassy swale or in the bunker. I'd prefer to be in the swale because I can run it out of there with a putter, but the back bunker is not difficult if you catch a decent lie. The trick here is to select the right club. As I was telling my nephew, J.C., a lot of times you face the hole on the tee with the wind coming over your left shoulder and you think the shot is downwind. Actually it may be blowing against you at the green. The wind comes whipping down Rae's Creek and swings around those pine trees and then comes back over your shoulder. I always make sure I've got half a club more than I think I need.

Tom Watson says the 12th green is really like three greens. I'll go at the flag when it's on the left side or even in the middle, but I won't go at the hole when it's cut on the right side. It's at least a club longer carry to the right part of the green, and if you miss, the penalty is more severe because the ground slopes sharply down to the hazard.

How you should play it: You have to play No. 12 pretty much the way I do, only forget about where the flag is. Your main objective is to get on the dance floor. Your green zone is the left half of the green; yellow is long and/or the right side of the green; red is short. Work hard on getting the right yardage and selecting a club that realistically will get you there.

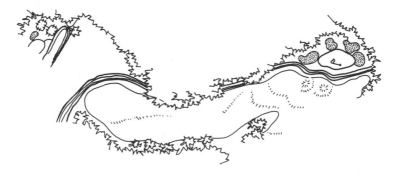

No. 13, par 5, 465 yards.

How I play it: The tee shot here is important for a pro because it means the difference between getting on in two or three. Where you don't want to hit your drive is left, either in the trees or in the creek or both. I've been in that SOB plenty of times, and you're lucky to escape with a bogey. The ideal driving spot is a little uphill ridge on the left side of the fairway—it helps get the second shot up in the air—about 220 yards from the green. The acceptable yellow zone, of course, is the right side of the fairway; I'd have to lay up from there.

If I'm going for the green on my second, where I don't want to hit it is right, as Curtis Strange did in the 1985 Masters. He ended up down in Rae's Creek, and that costs at least a shot and it helped lose him the tournament. If I'm going to miss my second, I want to miss it left. There's a swale and a couple of bunkers on the left side, but at least I have a chance to get down in two.

If I'm going to lay up my second, I prefer to go ahead and hit it as close to the creek as I safely can. I know some fellows prefer to lay up way back to hit a full shot with spin into the green, but unless the pin is cut very close to the front I'd rather play a half-pitch shot on my third.

How you should play it: This is a wide-open hole for you with nothing to fear. Your target off the tee is the right side of the fairway to the right rough. A good drive in that direction will kick around to the left, bringing you closer to the green. The yellow zone is down the middle, and the red zone is anything left.

If the flagstick is in the back of the green, you want to lay up your second shot short and left, so you have the full length of the green to shoot at. If it's in the front of the green, try to lay up long and right, again giving yourself more green to work with on the third shot. If you're getting a handicap stroke here, it should be money in the bank.

Allow me to pass along one final message before we get off the subject of course strategy. All this high-minded figuring isn't worth a used golf glove if you don't know how far you hit each club in your bag.

A fellow I used to play with every winter at Seminole in Florida taught me the value of knowing my distances, and it was one of those lessons that stuck. Whenever he had a big money match, this old boy got to the club at daybreak and volunteered to go out and set the tee markers on all the holes. He was really interested only in the markers on the par 3s. His best club in the bag was the 6-wood; he knew that rain or shine he could hit it 165 yards. Naturally he set all the white markers, where he played, so the par 3s played 165 yards. While his opponents were scratching their heads about what club to hit, my man had no doubts. I don't endorse his actions by any means, but I do admire his mastery of club selection.

One of the best innovations to come along in my lifetime is playing golf by yardage. We used to judge distance strictly by sight and feel. Now all the pros know exactly how far they hit each club and their caddies chart courses the way Rommel mapped North Africa. It's really helped me to continue playing as my eyesight has grown worse.

I've got what they call "deterioration of the retina" in my right eye, and glasses or operations or diets won't cure it. I have no depth perception at all; it's as if I'm looking out of one eye. My long game isn't affected because I know my distances, but my short game—inside 60 yards—has gone to hell. The pitch shot is the worst; I'm playing from memory now. I'm just so grateful that I learned to play by yardage, and I commend it to you as the only way really to play the game today.

If you don't know how far you hit each club, start pacing off shots during your next round and note the distances on a separate scorecard. After a couple of rounds, you should have a good idea of the yardage for almost every club in your bag. Tom Watson recommends pacing off your ball marks on a wet day; that way you get to learn how far your ball carries with each club, which obviously is critical on shots over trouble.

It's fine to rely on your caddie for distances when playing a strange course, but ask him only for the yardage, not the club selection. If you're unsure, consult him, but don't blindly take whatever club he suggests. I made this mistake at Pinehurst several years ago. On one hole I asked my caddie what club he thought I should hit.

"Seven-iron," he said, with conviction.

I hit it 10 yards past the hole, into the back fringe. On the next hole, I asked him again for his club selection.

"Three-iron," he said, again with authority.

This one finished 20 yards past the hole. "I don't think you're giving me the right clubs," I said, a little peeved.

"Mr. Snead," he replied, "all that goes to prove is that two heads would be better than one."

Appendix I

How to Mark a Scorecard

The scorecard is your friend. It keeps your opponents honest. Used correctly, it can put food on the table. Used incorrectly or not used at all, it can make you go hungrier than a woodpecker with a headache.

The first rule of betting is to write down all the bets on the back of the scorecard and repeat them to your opponent before teeing off. Some golfers have a tendency to forget lost bets. This eliminates any arguments after the round.

Always keep your own card. If an opponent offers to mark the scores, that's fine, but double-check his tally with your own. And triple-check any scorekeeper who uses a pencil with an eraser.

When filling out a scorecard on the first tee, put each player's handicap after his name. Then determine where the handicap strokes fall. On the scorecard below, Sam has a 10-handicap, Ben an 18, Jack a 12 and Arnie a 14. They are playing their matches off the low handicapper, so Sam gets no strokes, Ben gets 8, Jack 2 and Arnie 4. Most golfers indicate the stroke holes in one of three ways: small dots in a corner of each box, slashes or circles.

Hole	Handicap	MEN Blue	Par	White	Par	SAM 10	BEN 18	+	JACK 12	ARNIE 14		Par	WOMEN Handicap	Red
1	9	394	4	381	4							4	6	368
2	3	412	4	403	4		•			◯		4	4	332
3	13	283	4	278	4							4	16	272
4	15	198	3	190	3							3	8	166
5	1	576	5	550	5		•		/	◯		5	2	469
6	11	369	4	362	4							4	10	355
7	7	425	4	416	4		•					5	12	360
8	17	141	3	136	3							3	18	128
9	5	450	4	425	4		•					4	14	275
Out		3248	35	3141	35							36		2725
10	12	375	4	366	4							4	11	355
11	16	191	3	172	3							3	17	147
12	4	476	5	434	4		•			◯		4	5	367
13	10	438	4	408	4							4	7	358
14	8	408	4	396	4		•					5	9	332
15	14	222	3	213	3							3	13	202
16	2	525	5	488	5		•		/	◯		5	1	459
17	6	491	5	480	5		•					4	3	358
18	18	192	3	184	3							3	15	145
In		3318	36	3141	35							35		2723
Tot		6566	71	6282	70							71		5448
Hcp														
Net														

U.S.G.A. Rules govern all play.
Out of Bounds—on or across pavement of State Highway
White stakes—Out of Bounds
Red stakes—Lateral Water Hazard
Yellow stakes—Water Hazard

MEN
Blue—73.9
White—72.6
Red—69.1
WOMEN Red—71.6

Date: _____
Scorer: _____
Attested: _____

Scorecards reprinted courtesy Nationwide Golf & Printing Plant, Inc., Fayetteville, NC (919) 483-5746
© 1984 Nationwide Golf & Printing Plant, Inc.

In this hypothetical match, Sam and Ben are playing Arnie and Jack. As the match progresses, the running total is kept in the bottom row of boxes. They are playing automatic 2-down presses (see page 110), so each time either team goes 2 up in a match, a new bet starts. The scorekeeper keeps track of the presses in the running total. Sam and Ben win the first hole; they are +1. Sam and Ben win the second hole; they go +2, and a press starts. Sam and Ben lose the third hole; they stand 1 up in the original match and 1 down in the press, so the running tally is +1-1. Sam and Ben lose the fourth hole; they go even in the original, 2 down in the press, and another press starts. The running tally is 0-2. Then Sam and Ben win the fifth hole, so they stand 1 up in the original match, 1 down in the first press and 1 up in the second press; the running tally reads +1-1+1. And so on.

Hole	Handicap	MEN Blue	Par	White	Par	SAM 10	BEN 18	- +	JACK 12	ARNIE 14		WOMEN Par	Handicap	Red
1	9	394	4	381	4	4	5	+1	5	6		4	6	368
2	3	412	4	403	4	5	5°	+2	5	6°		4	4	332
3	13	283	4	278	4	5	4	+1 -1	4	3		4	16	272
4	15	198	3	190	3	4	4	0 -2	3	4		3	8	166
5	1	576	5	550	5	5	5°	+1-1+1	7°	6°		5	2	469
6	11	369	4	362	4							4	10	355
7	7	425	4	416	4			•				5	12	360
8	17	141	3	136	3							3	18	128
9	5	450	4	425	4			•				4	14	275
Out		3248	35	3141	35							36		2725

U.S.G.A. Rules govern all play.
Out of Bounds—on or across pavement o State Highway
White stakes—Out of Bounds
Red stakes—Lateral Water Hazard
Yellow stakes—Water Hazard

MEN
e—73.9
te—72.6
d—69.1
N Red—71.6

If you're playing "garbage," or side bets, you can keep track of the units won by putting a dot or slash next to the player's name. A more accurate system of tracking side bets is to use a second scorecard. Mark each name but leave the hole boxes blank until a player wins a point. Then on the back of the scorecard create your own code. For instance, say you're playing birdies (B), greenies (G), sandies (S), Arnies (A) and Hogans (H). See the glossary on page 105 for the definitions. If Sam makes a sandie on the first hole, put an S in his box on Hole No. 1. If Ben wins a Hogan and a birdie on the second hole, put an H and a B in his box on No. 2. It may sound a bit cumbersome, but the second scorecard is easy to keep once you're accustomed to the code and it accurately counts the side wagers. Give it a try.

Appendix II

USGA Policy on Gambling

(Excerpted from the Rules of Golf.)

The Definition of an Amateur Golfer provides that an amateur golfer is one who plays the game as a non-remunerative or non-profit-making sport. When gambling motives are introduced, problems can arise which threaten the integrity of the game.

The USGA does not object to participation in wagering among individual golfers or teams of golfers when participation in the wagering is limited to the players, the players may only wager on themselves or their teams, the sole source of all money won by players is advanced by the players and the primary purpose is the playing of the game for enjoyment.

The distinction between playing for prize money and gambling is essential to the validity of the Rules of Amateur Status. The following constitute golf wagering and not playing for prize money:

1. Participation in wagering among individual golfers.

2. Participation in wagering among teams.

Organized amateur events open to the general golfing public and designed and promoted to create cash prizes are not approved by the

USGA. Golfers participating in such events without irrevocably waiving their right to cash prizes are deemed by the USGA to be playing for prize money.

The USGA is opposed to and urges its Member Clubs, all golf associations and all other sponsors of golf competitions to prohibit types of gambling such as: (1) Calcuttas, (2) other auction pools, (3) pari-mutuels and (4) any other forms of gambling organized for general participation or permitting participants to bet on someone other than themselves or their teams.

The Association may deny amateur status, entry in USGA Championships and membership on USGA teams for international competitions to players whose activities in connection with golf gambling, whether organized or individual, are considered by the USGA to be contrary to the best interests of golf.

Glossary of Betting Games

Arnies. A side bet in which a unit is won by never having your ball in the fairway during the play of a hole and still scoring a par or better. Named for the legendary scrambler.

Backgammon. (Also called Double.) A wager between two sides in which each hole is played for a set amount that can escalate. At any point during the play of a hole, either side may double the bet. The opponent must accept or concede the hole. If the advantage switches as the hole progresses, the opponent may double back. (A golfer who doubles cannot do so again until his opponent doubles.) The doubling may continue until the hole is completed. For example, if Jack and Arnie are playing $1 backgammon and Jack hits his tee shot on a par 3 into a bunker, Arnie is likely to double. Jack can concede the hole or accept Arnie's double (accepting would mean that the hole is now being played for $2). Arnie then hits his tee shot into heavy rough, Jack walks up and inspects his opponent's lie and redoubles Arnie, who accepts, making the hole worth $4. Jack hits his sand shot four feet away and Arnie pitches to within five feet. Arnie makes his putt, leaving himself in the ideal backgammon position. He doubles again with nothing to lose. The best Jack can do is tie; he either must pay off $4 or gamble $8 on making the putt, with nothing to gain if it goes in. This game should be played with handicap strokes.

Barkies. A side bet in which a unit is won by hitting a tree during the play of a hole and still making a par or better. Your fellow competitors in the group must hear it hit timber; leaves do not count. Double Barkies, worth two units, are earned by hitting two trees on two different shots and still making a par or better.

Best-Ball. A match in which one golfer plays against the better ball of two or the best ball of three players.

Bingle-Bangle-Bungle. Three points are at stake on each hole: one for the first player to hit his ball on the green, one for the ball nearest the hole after all players are on the green, and one for the first ball into the hole. All putting is done according to who's away, marking after each putt. On par-3 holes, no point is awarded for the first ball on the green; this point goes to the second-closest to the hole after all are aboard. Each point is worth a set amount and you pay off after the round. It's a good equalizer to play in a group with a wide range of handicaps.

Birdies. A side bet in which units are awarded for each hole played in one under the par.

Bloodsome. A variation of foursomes play in which two play against two with both partners driving, but the opponents select the one drive to be played out in alternate shots.

Bridge. On each tee a bid is taken to determine which side controls the wager. The bid is what the partners bet they will score (net) on the hole; in four-ball matches, the bid is the predicted total scores of both players. Flip a coin for the opening bid on the first tee; thereafter, the first bid on each tee is made by the winner of the previous hole. After the opening bid, the opponents have three options: accept the bid as is, accept the bid but double the bet, or bid a lower number themselves (in which case the other side has the same three options). The wager doubles for every stroke more than one above or below the winning bid. Let's say, for example, the game is played for $1-a-stroke. If the team with the bid finishes one stroke above its number, it pays off $1; two strokes above, $2; three strokes above, $4; four strokes above, $8, and so on. If the team with the bid finishes with a total equal to the bid, it's a push (no one collects). If the bidders are one stroke below their number, they collect $1; two strokes below, $2; three strokes below, $4; four strokes below, $8, and so on. Play this game cautiously. Most payoffs are made when a team goes over rather than under its bid.

Carpets. (Also called Wall-to-Wall.) If a golfer or team wins every par-3 hole, the payoff is doubled.

Carryovers. When a hole is tied, the bet is carried over through subsequent holes until there is a winner. The eventual winner collects the total of whatever was wagered on the previously tied holes plus the one won. For example, if two teams are playing $1-a-hole carryovers, the first four holes are tied and then one team wins the fifth hole, the winning side collects $5.

Chapman Foursomes. (Also called The Pinehurst System.) A two-man team format in which both partners drive from every tee, then play each other's ball for one shot; then they decide which one ball to play, pick up the other ball and hit alternate shots into the hole.

Chicago. A system of handicapping in which each player is given a point quota based on his handicap (a 1-handicapper gets 38 points, a 2-handicapper gets 37 points, and so on). Each player then receives one point for a bogey, two points for a par, four for a birdie and eight for an eagle. The player who scores the most points over his quota wins the bet.

Fairways and Greens. A game for low handicappers, you get a point each for hitting the fairway off the tee (on par 4s and 5s) and for hitting the green in regulation. The scorekeeper records the points on each hole. You can either pay off on a per-point basis or winner takes all.

Flaggy. A side bet in which a unit is awarded for hitting your tee shot on a par 3 within flagstick distance of the hole.

Four-ball. A team match in which two golfers play their better ball against the better ball of the two others, with each golfer playing his own ball.

Foursomes. A match in which two golfers play against two others, and each side plays one ball. It generally refers to a straight alternate-shot format; one player hits the tee shot, his partner hits the second, and so on in rotation until the ball is holed. Partners rotate hitting tee shots regardless of who putted last.

Garbage. A common expression meaning all the additional side bets being played apart from the main wager on the match.

Greenies. A betting unit awarded on par 3s to the player closest to the hole on the green in one shot. In team competition, a greenie by a player earns the unit for his team. Sometimes it's played that a golfer loses the greenie if he takes more than two putts, but such variations must be made clear on the first tee.

Greensome. A foursome game in which two play against two with both partners driving; then they select one ball to play, finishing the hole in alternate shots.

Gruesome. A bet that requires a player to hit two balls on each shot (from the same position, not at the same time), and his opponent picks which ball will count each time. The usual wager is that a low handicapper cannot break 100 under this format. High handicappers should not even consider the bet no matter what over/under number is offered. (See Bloodsome for team variation.)

Hawk. (Also called The Boss.) A game played in a group of four golfers in which a batting order is established on the first tee. After all have hit their tee shots, the player who drove first decides who will be his partner on that hole. He has the option of picking any one of his three fellow competitors as a partner or choosing to play against their best ball on his own. If he plays alone, he has the opportunity to win or lose three units, collecting from or paying the other three. If he takes a partner, each player on a winning side collects one unit. The honor of being the first to drive (known as the Hawk) rotates on a 1-2-3-4 basis. The player who is down the most units after 16 holes becomes the Hawk on 17, and whoever is down the most after that hole has the honor on 18.

Hogans. A side bet in which a unit is won by playing a hole in regulation and never having your ball out of the fairway. Ben would like this game. (When played in conjunction with Arnies worth one unit, Hogans should have a higher value of two units.)

Honest Johns. A simple wager in which you pay off every other player in your group for each stroke you take; obviously the low scorer collects from everybody and the high scorer bums a ride home.

Kicker's Replay. A stipulation made on the first tee that allows each player to replay two shots in an 18-hole round; he must continue with the replayed ball.

Low Ball, Low Total. A four-ball game in which two points are at stake on each hole, one for the low ball and one for the low team total. In case of ties, no point is given.

Low-High. A four-ball game in which two points are at stake on each hole, one for the team with the low ball and one for the team whose high score is lower than the high score of the other team. In case of ties, no point is given.

Moles. A side bet in which the golfer who leaves his ball in a bunker after one shot must pay his fellow competitors one unit; if he leaves it in again, two units, and so on.

Nassau. The most common bet on a golf match, the basic nassau is played for three points: one for the front nine, one for the back nine, and one for the 18-hole match. The winner may be decided under several forms of play, but usually it is four-ball match play. Some golfers play a four-point nassau, with either the back nine or the 18 worth two points. Snead recommends a six-point nassau: one point for the front nine, two points for the back nine and three points for the 18. Make sure you call the terms on the first tee.

Nicklauses. A side bet in which a unit is won for having the longest drive in the fairway on each hole.

Nine-Point Game. The ideal betting game for a threesome, devised by P. Hal Sims, the master bridge player. Nine points are at stake on each hole. The best ball gets five points, the second best three, and the last place one point. In case of a tie, divide the points accordingly. If there's a two-way tie for low ball, the low players each get four points (5 + 3). If there's a two-way tie for second low ball, those players get two points apiece (3 + 1). If there's a three-way tie, each player collects three points.

Press. (Also called A Push, A Bump or "Roll the Drums.") A bet made during a match in addition to the original wager by the currently losing player, or side. The press runs only for the holes remaining to be played on a nine at the point the bet is declared. Although local rules vary, a press is usually not allowed unless the losing team is at least 2 down. The team ahead is not bound to accept the press, but it is customary. Another common local rule is that the press must be made immediately upon going 2 down in the match, which would prevent a player from waiting until he's getting a handicap stroke before calling the press. Snead recommends playing automatic presses, which means that a press bet automatically starts each time a side goes 2 down. (See Chapter 8 for further explanation and advice concerning press betting.)

Ransom. (Also called Six, Six and Six.) A two-man team game in which each side plays four-ball on the first six holes (with the better ball of the two counting), foursomes on the second six holes (playing alternate shots), and aggregate score on the last six holes (each playing his own ball and totaling their scores). Advocates of this game claim it can be played without handicaps as long as teams are roughly equal.

Reject. (Also called Wipe-Out.) A stipulation made on the first tee in which each player has the right to make his opponent replay four shots during a round.

Round-Robin. (Also called The Six-Hole Switch.) A game played for four players in a group who switch partners every six holes, with each six-hole match counting as one unit. For example, Players A and B are partners on the first six holes against C and D; A and C are partners for Holes 7 through 12 against B and D; A and D play B and C for the last six. A good sociable game, but like wild cards in poker it's not played by serious bettors.

Sandies. A side bet in which a unit is won by getting up and down in two shots for a par or better from a bunker. In team play, an individual wins the sandy for his side. An interesting variation is played at Lakeside Golf Club in North Hollywood, Calif., where a regular sandie from a greenside bunker is worth one unit; an up and down from a fairway bunker called a Super Sandie is worth two units; making a par on a hole where you have been in both a fairway and greenside bunker, an Exotic Sandie, worth five units.

Scramble. (Also called Swat or Captain's Choice.) A format in which teams comprise two or more players. Each player hits a tee shot, and then the best ball is selected for the next shot. Each member then plays from this spot, and the process is repeated until the hole is played out. Another variation is the American Airlines Scramble, named for an annual pro football-baseball tournament, in which each player on a four-man team must use his tee shot a minimum of four times. The Bogie Busters Scramble, named for a celebrity event in Dayton, Ohio, employs a variation in which low handicappers (scratch to 4) play from the back tees, middle handicappers (5 to 12) the middle tees, and high handicappers (13 and up) the front tees. Another format prohibits a player whose ball is selected from hitting the next shot.

Skins. (Also known as Scats or Skats.) A form of individual betting in which a player wins a unit by making the uncontested low score on a hole. If two or more tie for the low score, all tie. Skins generally are played at scratch— that is, without handicap strokes.

Snake. A game between individuals in a group, with wagering on every hole or in nine-hole increments. The first player who three-putts gets the snake. If betting is on every hole, he owes each fellow player a unit. The snake does not change hands until someone else three-putts. If nine-hole bets are being played, the player holding the snake on the ninth and 18th hole pays the other players. The snake is not a recommended game, because it slows down play as every golfer has to putt out.

Stableford. A scoring system popular in Britain but rarely used in the U.S. that awards points for scores on each hole as follows: 1 for a bogey, 2 for a par, 3 for a birdie and 4 for an eagle. The highest number of points scored decides the winner.

Three-Ball. A match in which three golfers play against one another, each playing his own ball.

Threesome. A match in which one golfer plays against two others, and each side plays one ball.

Umbrella. A collection of side bets in addition to regular team matches, with six points at stake on each hole: one for closest to the pin in regulation (in one on par 3s, two on par 4s, three on par 5s), one for low ball, one for fewest combined putts, one for birdies and two for low team total. If a team wins all six points on a hole, it's called an umbrella, worth double points.

Vegas. A four-ball betting game in which every player's score counts. To get your team score, combine the two individual scores putting the lower number first; for example, if A has a 3 and B has a 5, their team score is 35. The low team total wins, with the winning team getting the point difference between their score and their opponent's; for example, if A-B have a 35 and C-D have a 46, the A-B team wins 11 points (46 - 35). You can either play a set amount bet on each nine holes or a per-point wager. One variation allows a team scoring a birdie on a hole to reverse the opponents' combined number. If A-B had made a birdie in the above example, C-D's 46 would be reversed to 64 and the point differential would be 29 (64 - 35).

Watsons. A side bet in which a unit is won by holing a shot from off the green.

Wolf. A game played by a group of three golfers in which the player with the middle-length drive on par 4s and 5s and with the second closest to the pin on par 3s is known as the Wolf. He takes twice his score on a hole and matches it against the combined scores of the other two players.

Yardages. Points are won according to the length of holes on the scorecard. For example, a 395-yard par 4 is worth 395 points. Just keep track of who wins each hole on the course; leave the higher mathematics to the 19th hole.